COLUMBIA COLLEGE CHICAGO

P9-ARA-436

DATE DUE

DISCARD

Demco, Inc. 38-293

APR 1 1 2011

DRIVING
EXCELLENCE

Columbia College Library
600 South Michigan
Chicago, IL 60605

DRIVING EXCELLENCE

TRANSFORM YOUR
ORGANIZATION'S CULTURE
—AND ACHIEVE
REVOLUTIONARY RESULTS

MARK AESCH

HYPERION

NEW YORK

Copyright © 2011 Mark Aesch

All rights reserved. No part of this book may be used or reproduced in any manner
whatsoever without the written permission of the Publisher. Printed in the
United States of America. For information address Hyperion, 114 Fifth Avenue,
New York, New York, 10011.

Library of Congress Cataloging-in-Publication Data has been applied for.

ISBN 978-1-4013-2397-4

Hyperion books are available for special promotions and premiums. For details
contact the HarperCollins Special Markets Department in the New York office at
212-207-7528, fax 212-207-7222, or e-mail spsales@harpercollins.com.

Book design by Meryl Sussman Levavi

FIRST EDITION

10 9 8 7 6 5 4 3 2 1

THIS LABEL APPLIES TO TEXT STOCK

We try to produce the most beautiful books possible, and we are also extremely
concerned about the impact of our manufacturing process on the forests of the world
and the environment as a whole. Accordingly, we've made sure that all of the paper
we use has been certified as coming from forests that are managed to ensure the
protection of the people and wildlife dependent upon them.

I will always work to make you proud.

ACKNOWLEDGMENTS

I spent the first twenty-one years of my life on a small family farm feeding cows and shoveling their output. People like me don't write books. We're lucky to be done putting hay in the barn early enough in the evening to even read one.

There wouldn't be a story to share were it not for my parents. Richard and Sandra Aesch taught me so many lifelong lessons on their 140-acre farm. Whenever work seems hard today, I remember what *real* work looks like. Serving farm animals breakfast before getting to open presents on Christmas morning emblazons in an eight-year-old's head what service to others really means.

A friend asked me recently what one single person, had he or she not been there over the last years at RGRTA, would have prevented us from achieving the breakthrough results that we have realized. My response: John Doyle, the chairman of our board. He challenged and inspired us, and he also stayed out of our way as we worked to achieve our mutual vision of running a public agency with a private-sector mind-set. Indeed, so many on our board and our management team demonstrated terrific strength and courage as we learned together the difference between tough decisions and sad ones.

My old boss, former United States Representative Bill Paxon, taught me so many lessons. I will always be grateful for the work Bill did for our nation and the lessons he taught so many young people, like me.

Next I must thank one of the finest elected officials I have ever observed, Monroe County executive Maggie Brooks. Confident, collaborative, and creative, Maggie is that rare public official who time and again places sound public policy above her personal politics. I've sat beside her as she makes decisions potentially harmful to her political future but right for the community. I am so proud of her work and more proud to have her as a lifelong friend.

Of course, the story of *Driving Excellence* is only possible because of our committed workforce of 825 dedicated professionals. Cleaner buses, improved on-time performance, fewer buses breaking down, and many other on-the-ground accomplishments have made possible our transition to serving *customers* rather than picking up passengers. Senior executives, mid-level and junior employees, bus drivers, maintenance workers, people in the call center, and folks in the service building all deserve immense credit for putting themselves out there and changing their thinking. I would specifically like to thank my executive assistant, April Jordan; our now former vice president of communication, Jacqueline Halldow; our budget manager, Chris Dobson; our chief financial officer, Robert Frye; and our general counsel, Hal Carter. These professionals, and so many of their colleagues, could manage nearly any private company in the nation. They are that good.

My Young Presidents' Organization (YPO) brothers provided a safe haven so many times over the past year as I struggled to write this book while keeping all the plates spinning. I will always be grateful to Brian, Gene, Chris, Mark, Scott, Steve, Dan, and Mike for their encouragement, counsel, and occasional kicks in the ass.

To incredibly dear friends like John Brown, Frank Contestabile, Shelly Dinan, Bill Nojay, and Dawn Palazzo—thank you! You helped and supported me, believing that the story of our work in Rochester could improve the quality of organizations across the country. Your excitement for this project inspired me to work that much harder.

Michael Abrashoff, the retired Navy captain and author of *It's Your Ship*, made time for me when he didn't even know me and I didn't know the first step to take. He opened that very first door, kicking off the transformation of this project from idea to reality. I can only hope I might someday return the favor to someone, making the time for them when my telephone rings.

Lorin Rees, my agent for this project, saw our story as one that needed to be told. What I presented to him at first was rough and unsophisticated, but he helped to polish it and constructed a path to make the delivery of this book possible. I will always be grateful to him for his vision and judgment.

Seth Schulman, my editor, has become a lifelong friend through this process. A magician with words, Seth took every concept and made it sharper, added vividness to every story, and gave life to the Little Bus Company That Could. His creative collaboration has been a gift.

The story of *Driving Excellence* is the story of hundreds of employees that made the transition from looking for a handout to getting up in the morning dedicated to excellence. Our success is theirs. And I am honored to share it with you.

Mark Aesch
Mayfield, NY
November, 2010

CONTENTS

DRIVING
EXCELLENCE

INTRODUCTION

The bus company I run in Rochester, New York, was once as beleaguered as any organization in America. When I was appointed CEO of the Rochester Genesee Regional Transportation Authority (RGRTA) in 2004, I received a nice opening day surprise—a massive $27.7 million budget deficit. Previous management had seen the crisis coming but hadn't taken steps necessary to avert it. Now, with a total budget of around $70 million, we were cooked. During my first weeks in the corner office, colleagues were advising me that we would survive only if we took not one but *all* of the following drastic steps: raising fares 40 percent across the board, reducing service by 65 percent, doubling fares on the disabled population we served, and axing about a quarter of our workforce.

We didn't do any of these things. Rather, we focused on transforming our business from the bottom up so that we could execute better. In two years' time, we turned that $27.7 million deficit into a $19.7 million *surplus*, a $47.2 million swing. Since then, it's only gotten better. For four years in a row, we've actually made money—more than $29.7 million and counting—while also growing our organization (our annual budget is now around $85 million). Since 2004, the number of people we carry has increased by more than 20 percent, a rate nearly 50 percent higher than the national average. Our routes today pick up more people for each mile we drive than they used to— over 50 percent more. Our buses are cleaner, and customer satisfaction, which had never before even been measured, is on the rise.

Oh, and try this on for size: In 2008, at a time of recession, when airlines were charging customers to bring luggage on board, FedEx was raising its delivery prices, and many public transit systems were pushing through not one but two fare increases, we actually *lowered* our fare—to just $1, a price not seen since 1991.

Government has underperformed for so long that people doubt any agency can achieve breakthrough success. Cynics talk about how inefficient government is as if that's a foregone conclusion. They are wrong. Government isn't inefficient. Things that are big are inefficient. Are you going to call Citibank efficient? Or General Motors? Big organizations create bureaucracy. They suck energy and stifle creativity.

This book shares the fundamental principles of the RGRTA's success in hopes of changing how organizations of all kinds operate. Forget the cynics; it *is* possible to take the rotten, dysfunctional, spendthrift organizations we've got and make them better. With careful and sustained effort, public agencies like hospitals, subway systems, schools, and police forces can execute efficiently and productively. The private sector, too, can eliminate the corruption buried in firms like Enron and Adelphia. With some good old-fashioned elbow grease, accountability and integrity on the part of management, and by applying the managerial principles outlined in this book, underperforming companies can remake themselves, just as we did.

Before 2004, we weren't much of a bus company. Like many public agencies, we had no far-reaching vision, just the pervasive notion that "this place pretty much runs itself," as the former CFO liked to say. What that meant was that finance ran everything in a reactive way. Unable to change with the times, and with no systems in place to even tell management what was changing, the company saw business stagnate year after year. Management's primary directive was to get service out on the streets at all costs, and so we had dirty buses puttering about behind schedule with one or two people bouncing around in back. An egotistical, paternalistic leadership—again, not that different from what exists at many agencies and other underperforming organizations—handed out goodies at its whim, and consequences for bad performance at any level of the organization were unheard of. Many managers operated on the assumption that they would get larger budgets next year, no matter how well they did. Predictably, they didn't do too well. Company morale was awful. Not knowing when to celebrate, the organization lacked vitality and energy. People talked about "getting their time in," as if they were in prison.

Step by wrenching step, we've transformed ourselves into a disciplined, dynamic, data-driven organization that is now the envy of our peers. Drawing inspiration from the private sector, we've dispensed with the "this place runs itself" philosophy and evaluate every corner of our business, reengineering entire processes and employing new technologies to get things done better, more efficiently, and with a reduced reliance on taxpayer subsidies. To assess our progress, we measure what matters using state-of-the-art tools that have raised eyebrows in the private sector. We seek transparency with regard to all constituents—our board, our employees, our customers, and the public. Internally, a culture of rigorous debate reigns, and when we succeed, we celebrate like crazy. As a result, our people not only want to work here; most of them put in their best effort each and every day.

Our organization is not perfect. We are neither geniuses nor saints. Every day, we check our egos and assumptions about how to do things at the door and focus with all our might on building a state-of-the-art, performance-based organization. If you manage a company, a public agency, or a not-for-profit, take heart—there's so

3

much you can do, starting today, to help your organization excel. If you're a taxpayer, a consumer, or a shareholder, I urge you to *demand* performance-based management in the organizations that take your money. If my own chronically dysfunctional organization can remake itself, on the brink of a total meltdown no less, then any number of institutions across America can, too. Taxpayers and the public at large deserve efficient government, while consumers deserve businesses that operate with a public servant's eye toward stewardship. We all deserve organizations that work again—organizations that drive excellence.

REDISCOVERING LEADERSHIP

The chapters ahead offer many lessons from our turnaround experience, but at the outset I'd like to highlight two fundamental macro-themes. The first is the importance of inspired and determined leadership. No matter what challenge we face, we can't fix organizations without people and their tremendous will to set aside the status quo, take risks, and do things differently. We need this determination not just on the part of a chief executive and the senior management team, but on the part of a broad number of individuals who are either selfishly motivated to save their jobs or organizationally motivated to operate more productively.

Walk into our executive suite today, or stroll through the mammoth garages where grease-covered mechanics take apart and rebuild entire buses, and you'll find the same thing: professionals who are not only dedicated to the organization's success, but who will speak up and fight for positive change when they believe it necessary. You wouldn't have found this kind of engagement several years ago. It's something we grew into. And as the CEO, I'll tell you right now, it's something *I* grew into.

Before I was appointed to lead the RGRTA, I had worked a variety of jobs: aide to a member of Congress, town administrator, staff member at RGRTA, and most recently, coordinator of a large public construction project. I had never run my own organization, and I had zero formal business training. Most of what I knew about leadership came from the commonsense wisdom my parents taught me on the small farm in upstate New York State, about an hour outside of Albany, where I grew up. You can imagine how daunting the fiscal crisis seemed to me during those early weeks. It was a defining test. Would my political know-how and down-on-the-farm wisdom be enough to guide this organization through? More importantly, would a newbie like me (I was only thirty-seven) be able to convince skeptical old-timers and entrenched interest groups to embrace the dramatic short-term changes we needed just to survive, let alone flourish?

Management had spent freely in recent years, and at the time that might have seemed like a safe thing to do. Unfortunately, those massive increases in expenditures were built on the rosiest economic conditions in history. When our revenue streams plummeted more than 40 percent to more historic norms, we found financial disaster on our doorstep. To make things worse, the price of diesel fuel, a relatively flat expense for years, was now skyrocketing.

I spent my first two months on the job working with our team trying to figure out what in the heck to do to prevent the roof from caving in. It looked like we wouldn't survive the year without a massive government bailout. We knew we needed to slash expenses, but I wanted to do it intelligently, saving us, if at all possible, from having to make heartbreaking layoffs and raising fares. After many late nights, considerable hand wringing, and not a little heartburn, we came up with a creative plan that called upon the whole organization to come together and reshape itself. We would adopt none of the traditional solutions. We would say no to fare hikes. No to slashing service. And no to massive layoffs. Instead, we would reorganize how we delivered service to the community so that we would operate more efficiently. We would do away with unproductive routes and work to increase the number of people we picked up, all in an effort to lower costs and increase income. As part of this plan, we would cut some sacred cows such as lucrative overtime pay; if everything went well, though, we wouldn't have to lay off any of our 750 employees, and we'd keep fares stable. Times would be tough, but there was a silver lining: With this plan in place, we would be positioning ourselves to ease our reliance on government handouts and become a better, more sustainable, performance-based organization over the long term.

We thought our plan would succeed, but we didn't know if we had enough time, and we didn't know if rank-and-file employees would cooperate. We were going to be asking a lot more of our drivers. Their buses were about to become much fuller; no more racing to the end of a route so they could read a newspaper or take a nap. After multiple meetings at which I made it clear we were facing a financial crisis, we announced elements of the plan. The response wasn't great. Previous management hadn't said anything about a fiscal crisis, and to the rank and file it looked like the new guy—me—had already screwed things up. We weren't proposing layoffs, but the union leadership still decided they hated me. I received vicious unsigned letters attacking and even threatening me. I was accused of everything from embezzlement, to having granted no-show jobs to political friends, to, my personal favorite, having had a hot tub installed on top of the administration building for my personal use. And on and on they howled.

OUR OWN LITTLE CAESAR

Tensions crested during a meeting when I announced details of our turnaround plan. We convened in a massive garage where we store about a quarter of our 410-bus fleet. Halogen lights hung from ceilings thirty feet high, and massive overhead doors opened on either end of the eight-lane, 150-yard-long concrete floor. At one end of the garage, we'd created a square using four of our red, white, and blue buses.

Dozens of our employees sat in the middle of this square on folding chairs. Behind them, dozens more angry mechanics, bus operators, and other union workers stood with arms folded across their chests; they felt that if they stood in the back, they would be on equal footing with me, since I was standing at the other end of the space. These union workers were scary and thuggish, with tattoos, surly attitudes, foul mouths, and serious muscles. And they were livid. Why, all of a sudden, was this hotshot suit coming in to take away their perks?

The most threatening and angry union employee of them all was a 350-pound bus driver named Caesar McFadden. I'll always remember him. He probably stood six feet five inches and wore gold earrings and a heavy assortment of gold chains. Oh, and he wore a placard around his neck that read, in big block letters, "LIAR." I assumed he wasn't talking about himself.

I began the meeting by summarizing our situation. The organization was drowning and we needed to save ourselves. We were on the verge of not being able to meet payroll. If we didn't pull together, shift the bus schedules around, and provide our service in a far more efficient fashion, we'd soon need to take other, less palatable measures. I reminded our people that we didn't run buses in an effort to employ drivers. That was the old way of doing things. We ran buses because there were people to pick up. We ran buses to serve customers.

Union employees did everything they could to interrupt me. Grumbling, hissing, and expletives came from the back of the area. The same response greeted our twenty-five-year veteran vice president of scheduling, Chuck Switzer, when he tried to explain the new system we had built to figure out which routes were productive and which weren't. Things were getting ugly. The real fireworks started when I opened the meeting to questions. Caesar McFadden, standing in the back with his big "LIAR" sign, stuck up his hand. He looked me straight in the eye. "Are you telling me you're going to be laying a bunch of our people off because of this crazy thing you've come up with?"

I swallowed hard. "No. What I'm saying is—"

"So you're saying you're *not* gonna be laying any of us off," Mc-Fadden interrupted, sticking his chest out. Those around him hooted him on as he was challenging the boss.

I started up again. "What I was attempting to say is that—"

"You people don't give a damn about us!" McFadden shouted, pointing at me. "You don't know what we go through every day. You don't care about our bills. Our families." McFadden was really starting to whip it up now, playing to the crowd.

Every fiber of my being told me not to yield. When he paused to take a breath, I said, "You've asked a question. I would hope that you're actually interested in an answer. Now, what I was attempting to say—"

McFadden interrupted me again, but this time I wouldn't stand for it. "You asked a question," I said, raising my voice in anger. "I'm going to answer it. You will *not* interrupt me a fourth time!" There was no way I was going to let him take over our meeting and confuse employees with non-issues.

His chest deflated and his shoulders sank. He realized he had gone as far as he could. He and Frank Falzone, the union's business agent, stormed out, taking all the union employees with them. I laughed to myself at that point. The meeting had gone on for about an hour and it was basically finished. Yet I knew I couldn't let the meeting end because the bulk of the union employees had engaged in some silly walkout, as though that would somehow change the dire situation in which we all found ourselves. So I just made up stuff for ten minutes more so it would at least seem as though their departure hadn't brought an end to the meeting.

This episode was pivotal for me as a leader; it was then that I realized just what kind of unflinching stubbornness it would take to bring change in the face of groups and individuals with a perceived interest in resisting it. As we'll see later on, this wasn't a one-off strength I would have to show, nor would it be limited to times of crisis. I would need to muster a single-minded, day-in, day-out commitment to serving the organization's best interests no matter what.

Driving excellence is hard. Your most committed employees will question if you've gone too far. Pressure groups will attack you through the media, demanding that things be done *their* way, the public interest be damned. Every organization has its Caesar Mc-Faddens; in fact, every organization has many of them. Yet the forces of change must stand their ground and face down the loudmouths. Whatever else leadership is, it isn't a popularity contest. People in any position of responsibility must be prepared to make decisions every day that jeopardize their own personal interests so as to achieve the right outcome for their organization. Just as important, leaders need to encourage dissenting viewpoints, presenting the bad news as transparently as the good. Such integrity not only establishes the credibility you need to push through the tough decisions; it also inspires employees throughout an organization to work a little harder and expect others to do so as well—what we at the bus company call "demanding excellence."

The forces of change must stand their ground and face down the loudmouths. Whatever else leadership is, it isn't a popularity contest.

DRIVING A NEW HYBRID

Superior leadership is vital to remaking a dysfunctional organization, yet it is only part of the general picture this book will present. As time passed and the RGRTA moved from handling its immediate crisis to remaking every corner of its operations, we realized that we were evolving a new, hybrid model for managing that was unlike anything we had seen in either the public or private sectors—indeed, that melded the best in each. Our commitment to this model has been critical to our continuing success, and I'm describing it here in hopes that it can help public agencies and private companies alike remake themselves and exceed taxpayers' and shareholders' wildest expectations.

Most people don't talk about it, but there's a disease in government today. It's called incrementalism. Society changes and so do markets, but public-sector management contents itself with doing the same thing year after year, making only minor changes around the edges. Managers at schools, hospitals, water districts, and the like regard what they provide as an intangible and essential "service," the success or failure of which can't be measured. Since these organizations often operate with a monopolistic attitude, managers think nothing of providing service that very few people would actually choose to buy on the open market. They provide schools with decrepit buildings, hospitals with indifferent staff, airports with archaic technology, and in our industry, buses that are dirty and late. If you enjoy a captive audience, why excel as an organization? Why improve? "Take it or leave it" is management's unspoken attitude. It was our attitude for years.

That's not all. When determining their budgets, the main question most public managers ask is not "How can we innovate to make our existing dollars go further?" Rather it is "How much more money do we need next year to do the things we're doing now?" And the usual answer: "Four percent on top." That is, management will content itself with maintaining the status quo and providing the same mediocre service, yet they'll feel perfectly comfortable asking legislatures, and as a result the taxpayer, for 4 percent more each year to cover rising expenses due to inflation and market fluctuations.

We've succeeded because we've managed to throw "incrementalism" out the window and do the unthinkable: remake ourselves as a private company. Private companies have outperformed government agencies not because they possess superior leadership, but because market pressures force firms to innovate and improve their processes. Public organizations don't force those same pressures on themselves.

Since we wanted to optimize our execution, we resolved to take the best of what private companies do and adapt it to our business. This entailed a total change in how we viewed our operations and the language we used every day to describe them. We came to regard the people we served not as "passengers," as they had been called and treated for decades, but as *customers*. Likewise, our buses weren't merely vehicles for the transport of chattel; they were *movable stores*, and our drivers were *greeters*—like at Wal-Mart—with the mission of saying hello to customers at the front door, treating them well, and providing them with a superior experience, so that they would come back.

From this new way of thinking, a number of other steps followed. Like any business, we'd make decisions based on what customers were telling us, and on what our first-call employees perceived the customers wanted, not based on what political pressure groups said. In order to serve our customers, we'd watch our money very carefully; we'd need to know exactly how much it cost to make a wheel turn. We'd also take the lead from best-in-class private companies and develop clear, relevant ways to measure what we were doing and how we were performing.

Politicians talk all the time about running government like a private company. We don't just slap that on a bumper sticker. We actually do it. Yet privatizing our business wasn't the whole answer. As we've suggested, private sector managers are usually motivated to improve because of market demand. We were partially public servants, and as such we were motivated to improve not because the customer was clamoring and threatening to go elsewhere, but out of a sense of stewardship—because we thought it was important for the customer to have the very best product and value.

At the beginning of our turnaround, we spent a year examining our business and struggling with a basic question: Was our core responsibility to our customers, or was our core responsibility to the taxpayers who paid for part of our budget? Following the model of a private company, did we have an obligation to provide superior bus service to the community, or did we as a public agency have an obligation to maximize return to the taxpayer? The answer, we discovered, was . . . yes!

Like Starbucks or Best Buy, we had a responsibility to provide superior service if we wanted to get rich, but in the public interest we also had a responsibility to return as much value as possible to taxpayers. Serving both masters meant we needed to focus on *efficiency*—doing more good for our customers with the least amount of money from the public coffers. It sounds obvious, but nobody else was doing it. Focusing on efficiency led us to develop a nationally innovative service delivery model and corresponding measurement system to boost our productivity.

Think for a moment how powerful this balanced, two-pronged approach to management is. When almost any organization, public, private, or not-for-profit, cuts their service, their customer base falls off, and their remaining customers are less satisfied. When we, in our moment of crisis, made huge service changes, we reduced the total number of buses on the road by almost 12 percent. But since we focused on working smarter, with both a microscope and a scalpel, we actually wound up *increasing* both our customer base and customer satisfaction.

In 2004, every day we were picking up about 4,000 students who attended school in the city of Rochester, and we were losing sixty cents on the dollar for the privilege. Today, we pick up more than 11,500 students a day attending middle and high schools and fully cover our costs in a public-public partnership that is a model for other cities across the nation. More students are getting to class, school attendance is up, and the taxpayer is saving millions a year. Now, *that* is driving excellence.

We can summarize the management approach conveyed in this book by saying that we borrow the best practices from private sector companies and then, in an effort to make them even better, fuse them with a dedication to public stewardship. It's a more balanced approach applicable to organizations of all kinds. Many government agencies fail today because they serve neither taxpayers nor customers, but themselves. Yet many private firms also underperform because they show only a narrow-minded loyalty to shareholders. Many private sector managers would do far better if they took more seriously their broader corporate responsibility. It's not in a company's long-term interest to operate a grocery store at a 10 percent profit margin in a market with three competitors, while in a community with only a single grocery store chain, the company operates at a 30 percent margin. Yes, a firm in the latter situation clearly can and should charge more; it has a responsibility to make money. Yet to reap benefits like heightened customer loyalty and the intangibles that follow, private firms should "balance" community responsibility with shareholder return. And that can be built into a sustainable business model—with formulas—and ultimately measured. When the single grocery store chain faces competition, as it likely will, it will already find itself well positioned to sustain its customer base.

DRIVING EXCELLENCE

I've written this book because I know that we have built something magical in Rochester. While the entire industry was moving left, we moved right. Here we are, a public agency that is outperforming the private sector. We didn't just talk about productivity; we found a way to measure it and increase it by more than 90 percent. We **We figured out how to drive *fewer* miles and pick up *more* people who were *happier* riding.** didn't just talk about customer service, but found a way to measure that, too, and increase it by 16 percent. We were supposed to lose tens of millions of dollars, but instead wound up making tens of millions. We figured out how to drive *fewer* miles and pick up *more* people who were *happier* riding. At a time when government seems

MARK AESCH

poised to grow through taxpayer expenditures, bailouts, and private industry oversight, it is clear from the work we have done that there is a smarter choice.

The chapters that follow cover many dimensions of running a business. Each discusses an area of management, and each offers a lesson we learned through the often painful process of remaking our organization: Listen hard to employees as well as customers; don't let finance dictate your strategy; engage the entire organization in the new direction; create a culture of no-ego; and so on. Throughout the book, I strive to let employees share the limelight and give their perspectives on how *we* together turned this company around. I illustrate our arguments with real-life stories while also exposing readers to tools and techniques we've developed that have proved helpful to our success.

If you're one of those people content to "put 4 percent on top," then you shouldn't read this book. "Four percent on top" is a methodology for mediocrity and mere survival. Everyone is happy with "4 percent on top." Nothing changes. Status quo. Easy as pie. You will never face Caesar McFadden. But if you want to lead, transform, challenge, and spend every single day doing your level best to make the organization succeed, then this book is for you. Driving excellence isn't a pipe dream; what we accomplished can be realized in a police or fire department, a school district, a grocery store chain, a logistics company, a not-for-profit, even an entire state. Working together, we Americans can turn our bus around, one stop at a time. Take it from us, the little bus company that not only could, but *did*.

1.

NOBODY KNOWS
THE DRIVER'S NAME

Create a Culture of No Ego

I gazed out the drafty windows of my new office and watched rain splatter onto the parking area three stories below. It was a gray Sunday afternoon, and the lot was empty. I made a cup of tea and got to work on my first strategic task: organizing my office.

Go into many CEOs' offices, and you see pictures of them with celebrities or famous elected officials. You see elaborate artwork and richly carved furniture that evoke their personal wealth and power. You see awards they've won and diplomas they've earned.

When I became CEO in early April 2004, the first thing I did was decorate my office—in a very different style. I didn't put a single picture of myself on the walls, nor did I hang any awards or diplomas. I decorated my new office with Red Sox regalia I'd collected since the age of nine, as well as meaningful pictures I'd taken myself and had framed. I also rearranged the furniture to create a circle on the guest's side of my desk; that way, when a visitor came we could sit together and discuss the issue in a collaborative way. I wanted an office that broke the traditional power barrier. I wanted an environment that encouraged people to feel as if we were working together in solving problems— an environment that demonstrated that they had power, too.

I didn't know then many of the specific initiatives I wanted to advance or decisions I intended to make, but I did know I was committed to transforming this organization from one that seemed listless, fearful, and fragmented into one that was giving, selfless, and community-minded. I hoped, as best I could, to create a culture of no ego.

Why focus first on reforming the culture rather than on getting our financial house in order? Simple. Addressing the massive crisis that employees didn't even know existed would require a sea change not merely in processes or spending habits, but in how employees viewed everyday things like how we delivered service, how we communicated with each other, and how we viewed our own position in the broader community. People would have to venture beyond their comfort zones, take personal risks, and focus on improving their own performance. Along the way, we would have to pull together and make some pretty tough sacrifices for the good of the organization.

Attending to my own office décor, Red Sox memorabilia and all, was pivotal because cultural change had to start at the top. Employees wouldn't change their perceptions or take risks if they believed I was merely enjoying my own ego trip. Nobody wants to be a backdrop for another picture the CEO is hanging on his or her wall. By contrast, a CEO who from the first day puts employees ahead of personal prestige—now, that's inspiring! A positive change in the attitude of leadership hits at the foundation of a culture that formerly said "me first."

Nobody wants to be a backdrop for another picture the CEO is hanging on his or her wall.

Successful organizations, whether not-for-profits, private companies, or even sports teams, share one thing in common: an ability to get those at the so-called bottom of the organizational structure to believe that those at the top are furthering everyone's interests. When employees, board members, customers, taxpayers, or stockholders observe selfless actions on the part of senior managers, the entire organization experiences waves of selfless behavior and contributions at even greater levels. The culture changes, and the organization produces excellent and sustainable results, even in the face of changing conditions. My own organization's experience, which I'll relate in this chapter, is a case in point. It took time, and much more than symbolic decisions about office décor, but we did manage to transform our culture from the top down. And it has paid off on our bottom line.

$700 OFFICE CHAIRS AND FREE TURKEYS

If David Letterman came up with a list of the top ten most unhelpful behaviors of egotistical managers, what do you think would be on there? How about correcting a vice president when he didn't address you using "Mr."? Or sitting down each day in a $700, ergonomically designed office chair? Or telling assistants that they needed to "buy insurance" for their jobs by consulting with you before taking an action?

Today, some of our longtime employees remember precisely these behaviors over the years on the part of previous managers. It's not unusual—if you're like me, you can think of any number of bosses you've had (or perhaps still do have!) who have irritated you by nursing their inflated egos. Egotism is especially rife in public administration. In far too many hospitals, police departments, city halls, and the like, public servants **Public servants become excessively preoccupied with demonstrating that they're in charge rather than actually *being* in charge.** become excessively preoccupied with demonstrating that they're in charge rather than actually *being* in charge. The majority of such bosses aren't bad people with selfish motives. They tend to be older, products of a bygone age when more egotistical and authoritarian leadership styles were the norm.

When I became CEO, the old ways were still entrenched, as they had been for decades. As evidence, we still had a physical wall separating the executive suite from all the other administrative employees. The very fabric of life was dominated by senior leaders—their wills, their desires, their power, their personalities. As I realized, a me-first approach was leading to poor decisions that hindered day-to-day operations. Egotism was also filtering down the ranks, eroding employee loyalty, inspiring outright fear, and damaging performance.

Perhaps the most harmful expression of unrestrained egotism at our company involved established patterns of decision-making that were paternalistic and dominated by personality. At every level of our business, bosses liked to come across as warmhearted people who did good things for others. Any perks or benefits granted to the employees had to be seen as an expression of the manager's own big-heartedness. It was common for senior executives to go out to our expansive garages where we repaired and stored our hundreds of buses and hand out turkeys just before Thanksgiving. Not surprisingly, our bus drivers loved them for it. Employees would line up by the dozens to claim their free turkey.

At the local LPGA golf tournament, we used to set up an account at the welcome tent of a charity a senior executive was involved with so that any of our employees could go in, order anything they wanted to eat, and put it on the bus company's account. Likewise, we had a long tradition whereby the CEO personally heard one or two union employee grievances a week, deciding small things like whether a driver had received his or her proper overtime pay or whether managers had properly disciplined someone for a bad customer interaction. He would gather ten or so employees in the third-floor conference room, and the simplest hearing would last for an hour. Another tradition in our culture was that changes in salary for every employee, receptionists and vice presidents alike, went through the CEO.

Paternalism hurts an organization when it stands in for honest-to-goodness strategic decision-making—when the sole purpose of a decision is to demonstrate to the workforce who's in charge. Rather than focus on big picture items, such as how efficiently we delivered service, previous managers spent dozens of hours picking out bus driver uniforms, and leadership team meetings were too often devoted to such critically important topics as what color our bus stop sign poles should be painted. A senior human resources executive should have spent her time managing our multimillion-dollar union contract affecting hundreds of employees. Instead, she involved herself in petty disputes with lower-level employees who in her view had usurped her authority.

At every level of our company, far too much spending was ego-based, haphazard, and purposeless. Consider just one decision we made about putting service on the street. One senior executive had a friend who lived outside our service area, in an apartment complex where many people with disabilities lived. Without a larger plan in place, this executive decided we would run on-demand buses there. No one challenged that order, even though the staff knew it was wrong. Unfortunately, the directive to run these buses cost the organization hundreds of thousands of dollars over the years. Never mind if those scarce dollars were needed in other parts of the business more vital to the organization's long-term health or that served the organization's mission better.

I'm not trying to pillory senior executives at the Authority going back years prior. It's not as if I've never made a decision with paternalistic overtones. It's when such behavior defines a culture that you run into trouble. On too many occasions, our company took pity on people with sad stories and hired them for makeshift jobs. Over time, such charity cases abounded, representing a substantial leakage of money. And that wasn't the worst of it. Many of our company's ego-based decisions were so impracticable that employees didn't pay attention. When bus cleanliness became an issue, one executive handled it by gathering a large group of employees out in the garages where the repair work on buses was being done and complaining about how unhappy he was that the buses were so filthy. Employees' heads dropped as the attack continued. Then the bombshell. The executive proclaimed that any bus driver assigned a dirty bus was hereby authorized to refuse to drive that bus off the property.

Now, that sounds like a really cool, hard-line stance for a leader to take. And in fact, it did make that executive look good for the moment in front of the drivers. They howled with delight, slapping their thighs with the thought of not having to drive that day. Yet the directive was not actionable. As Bruce VandeWater, one of our veteran drivers, remarks, "Customers needed buses, even dirty ones, to get where they needed to go." So in practice everyone ignored the order. The problem wasn't fixed. The buses didn't get cleaner. Performance didn't improve. The executive got a short-term ego boost from projecting authority in front of dozens of employees, but over the long term it cost the organization—because nothing changed.

On another occasion, a senior leader decided that our company should have smaller buses. He then, appropriately, turned it over to his staff to decide which models to buy. After months consulting with mechanics, drivers, and bus manufacturers, analyzing all the information and scrutinizing the budget, the staff arrived at a recommendation. A big meeting was scheduled that brought together all the staff members who had invested dozens of hours in this process. They gathered in their boss's office to present their findings. "They don't look like buses," he proclaimed, from his position sitting behind his desk. "Bring me the catalogues!" They did, and he flipped through a few. "Now, those *look* like buses," he said, pointing to a certain model. "Buy those!"

"WE AIN'T GIVING NOTHING BACK"

The rooting of power in managers' personalities fostered a culture of pleasing. Yes-men and yes-women abounded, from the bus mechanics on up. Disagreement was not welcome. Debate didn't exist. The truth became an endangered species. Even identification of the challenges

20

themselves occurred only as a by-product of managers' whims. Yet you couldn't blame the employees. In an organization where decisions turned on the basis of a leader's emotions rather than on strategies and objective performance metrics, you did well by cultivating those emotions. As Myriam Contiguglia, a mid-level member of our communications team, notes, "It was rational back in the day to please the bosses; anything else was toxic to your career. It was exhausting. Every day, bad decisions were made by people in charge who didn't really know what was going on."

With the indiscriminate passing around of goodies, self-centered behavior became an especially unfortunate fixture of life at the Authority. Remember the welcome tent at the LPGA golf tournament? Drivers would pull into the half-moon loop with a full load of customers, let them off, pull their buses off to the side, and walk over to the charity tent to eat multiple hot dogs. "You wouldn't believe it," says Ryan Gallivan, a mid-level employee at the time in our Scheduling Department. "We'd have all kinds of buses stacked up with hundreds of people in line. It was really frustrating to have empty buses sitting there that should have been transporting our customers." Paternalism is exactly what creates a culture of me first.

The atmosphere at our Christmas party, held in the heated section of our bus garage, said it all. There was no spirit of fellowship or giving here. Since executives used to encourage employees to bring their families and friends, employees would walk in with six, seven, or eight people; all of them would grab what they could and then hustle out as fast as they could, foil-covered platefuls of ribs piled up in both arms. Although a small thing, the degeneration of the Christmas party epitomized so much of what was rotten with our organization. Our executives might have felt that they were giving ribs out of the goodness of their hearts, and no doubt they really did mean well. But such gestures also amounted to expressions of power and authority. Senior managers seemed to exist to give things away. All good things came through them. At their will. Ribs, salary increases, and "insurance."

In a company of turkey hoarders, you wouldn't expect the worker's union to jump at the chance to make reasonable concessions for the sake of the organization's survival. And in fact the union didn't. For years before I arrived, the union leadership's attitude was like everyone else's: Take, don't give. In other words, exploit every opportunity to grab anything you can from the organization. This attitude of the union's was never more apparent than during the first months of my tenure, when we were trying to figure out how to keep the ship afloat (or in our case, the bus running). We were doing our damndest to avoid laying off any employees. We decided to take one more shot at diplomacy with the union leadership in an effort to secure minor concessions from everyone and avoid having anyone lose his or her job.

Our new director of labor relations, Debbie Griffith, put hours into a one-page memo that laid out the financial crisis we faced and explained how with reforms to some ridiculous work rules and minor changes in health insurance plans we could operate more efficiently and save money, perhaps reducing the need for layoffs or a reduction in overtime. Then we had a meeting with union leadership. It took place on a Friday afternoon, in our third-floor conference room. They strutted in like they owned the place and helped themselves to refreshments. The meeting itself lasted just a few minutes. The president of the union took the single sheet of paper that Debbie had placed in front of him and tore it down the middle. "We ain't giving nothing back" were his words of wisdom. He wasn't holding a plateful of ribs, but you could almost smell them.

FEEDING THE COWS FIRST

It was clear we were going to have to transform this company from the bottom up. And to do that, we were going to have to change the culture. From the top down. Beyond redecorating my office walls with Red Sox paraphernalia rather than pictures of myself, I began my tenure by pushing that $700 office chair out into the hallway. I tried to remove the distance between myself and other employees by describing my upbringing shoveling cow manure and removing wagonloads of rocks from fields on our family farm. At my very first employee meeting, I made clear to employees that I grew up in an atmosphere where the cows got fed before the kids got to eat—that the world is about something bigger than ourselves.

Jim Holbert, a longtime employee who works on our buildings and grounds staff, had always made a point of addressing our CEO by "Mr." During my very first days on the job, I would correct him and ask him to call me Mark, but he would insist on calling me Mr. Aesch. He said he would do this to show his respect for me. I would explain that he showed his respect not by what he called me, but by showing up to work every day, doing his job well, and caring whether or not we were successful. We probably had this conversation once a month for several years before he finally began calling me Mark.

Undeterred by other initial resistance and setbacks, I hammered away that first year at the culture of me first by making symbolic decisions designed to reverse managers' egotistical concern with status. I not only demolished the physical wall that had separated the old corner office from everyone else; I also demolished the privileged attitude that members of our leadership team used to project in their personal work habits. Gone were the days when a senior leader could regularly stroll in at 9:45 in the morning or take a three-hour lunch. Now upper management had to work *harder* than everyone else, and I had to work hardest of all. That meant coming in at 7 A.M. and leaving after everyone else had signed off. Gone, too, were the days when a senior executive could say no to a subordinate and offer no other explanation other than their lofty position on the org chart. Now we had to respect the contributions of all our people and justify our answers on a rational basis.

THE CEO DOESN'T DO PARKING

We departed even more sharply from years past by phasing in a new, more participatory process of decision-making. Again and again that first year, I ceded control over areas of the business big and small that didn't require the CEO's direct attention. I made it clear that managers didn't issue "insurance premiums" any longer. This seemed odd to employees at first. I received a call from a bus driver as I sat working in my office one Saturday early in my tenure. The driver informed me that his boss, the deputy director of operations, had reprimanded him because he had parked his car in the wrong lot. The driver was calling me to find out where he was supposed to park.

"Are you seriously asking me this question?" I asked.

"Well, you're the CEO. You decide everything, right? Where am I supposed to park? What's your decision?"

I sat back in my chair and shook my head. "I don't do parking. If your boss says to park somewhere, then park there."

Beyond parking questions, I passed on resolving petty employee disputes. I've never presided over a low-level grievance hearing for union employees—not one. This is not to say that I don't meet with union employees when they have problems. Whenever any employee wants to meet with me, I make myself available. But here's the difference: My rule is that they can't bring union representation. The way I see it, I'm trying to resolve the employee's problem, not handle a union grievance behind the backs of our labor relations professionals. If an employee insists on having union representation, then that employee can handle the problem through the normal labor relations process. If the employee really wants to resolve the problem, he or she is welcome to meet with me alone.

That first year, we also ended the practice of having the CEO review all salary adjustments for administrative employees and deciding them on an arbitrary basis. From now on, people would be paid based on their performance as determined by objective metrics (more on that later in the book). The employees out front pulling on the tongue of the wagon and advancing our agenda would do better than those sitting in the back watching their colleagues struggle. In effect, this new policy pushed salary decisions down a rung in the hierarchy. Department heads would get a pot of money and dispense it as they saw fit. Only one rule: Each of the employees who reported to the department head couldn't receive the same salary adjustment. I wasn't about to let people off the hook by allowing them to give every member of their team the same adjustment in pay. Some people had worked harder than others, and they deserved more compensation.

Some of our department heads hated this new policy. For so long, our paternalistic approach had let them off the hook. "I would have happily gotten you more money," they used to say in hushed tones to their employees. "I think you're doing a great job. But *he* would only pay you this much. What am I supposed to do?" Some of the employees hated the new policy, too. They had gotten away with riding in the wagon, covered from the sun, for years now. Not anymore. We couldn't afford to sustain the rift between compensation and performance a moment longer. Extricating ego from decision-making would mean increasing all employees' responsibility for themselves and their reports—something we'll also explore in greater detail later on.

CREATING A TRUE LEADERSHIP TEAM

In giving up some of my oversight, I sought to empower our senior managers rather than keep them on as fawning yes-men. We repackaged our senior staff meetings, titling them "leadership team" meetings to emphasize the importance of teamwork and give them a new, more serious tone. We also changed their content. As I mentioned earlier, staff meetings had long been draining events. One or two department heads would report on a project, but for the most part our senior staff sat through ninety minutes or more of pointless conversation. These were your classic meetings without purpose; they took place not because we possessed information that merited discussion, but because it simply was the designated day of the month.

Under our new format, the agenda would pivot around a review of key measurement data and an assessment of how we were performing relative to our goals. I also did something that many around our large meeting table found awkward and terrifying. Influenced by Jim Collins's book *Good to Great*, I tried during my first year to encourage honest debate and disagreement among our leadership team. I asked colleagues to talk during meetings and contribute their wisdom. I solicited their critique of our policies and of my own ideas. I urged them to challenge me directly. And to challenge my conclusions.

This new format didn't work so well at first. Department heads stayed quiet, waiting for me to dominate. We would gather in the first-floor boardroom, blue chairs and matching floor-length drapes, and I would try hard to engage my colleagues, yet they would speak only when asked a direct question, and more often than not they wouldn't offer up a fresh insight. The fear of retribution historically ingrained into the culture was too great. After a few months, I grew frustrated. We had a solid agenda called Driving Excellence that we were trying to implement, but our meetings didn't push the ball forward; they were a total waste of time.

That first summer I wound up holding a special leadership retreat in a rustic cabin tucked away in the woods of Letchworth State Park, which has been repeated every year since. At the very end of the session, I introduced an exercise that I had purposefully not placed on the agenda beforehand. I asked each department head to go one at a time and disagree with something I had done over the prior five months of my tenure. Talk about uncomfortable! You could almost feel their blood pressures rising. But they did it.

The experience was a revelation for people. For the first time, they recognized they could disagree with the CEO, and nobody got yelled at or fired. Our team saw that *performance* mattered, and that from now on we were going to try to make things better rather than mollify the boss with happy talk. By the end of my first year, leadership team meetings began to improve. Today, our debates are fantastic, and our team maps out solutions that are better than anything any one of us could have come up with on his or her own. Given how animated team members get, outsiders would think we are fighting among ourselves. The reality is we are fighting to get to the best conclusion.

Some shared victories gave impetus to our emerging culture, proving that we could alter the way we do things and come out ahead. Two months after I took office, one of our larger customers, the Rochester Institute of Technology (RIT), told us that they were going to pull several hundred thousand dollars of subsidies they gave us every year to support our Route 24, which ran by their main campus. We had recently entered into a new five-year contract with RIT that had us losing money right out of the gate. Previous management made it clear to RIT that we would "do whatever it takes" to renew the relationship. Now our CFO, Bob Frye, was attempting to negotiate a business deal with the college. It's pretty difficult to negotiate a contract when you already have both your hands tied behind your back. But that's exactly the situation poor Bob Frye faced. Bob was a real pro who had spent years in senior financial positions spanning both the public and private sectors. His financial management skills were among the best in the business; he knew a good deal when he saw one. But he didn't always know how to listen. A physically imposing man in his mid-fifties, with thinning hair and a serious demeanor, Bob had enjoyed wide-ranging authority while serving as CFO under the former CEO. Now he was watching a bad deal that he had been forced to agree to replicate itself on Route 24. RIT was going to try to get the same deal on this service with the new CEO that it had gotten from the old CEO on the other service.

I, meanwhile, was in the midst of trying to make a difficult decision when it came to Bob. Because he had essentially served as CEO before I took office, I didn't think I could change the culture with him around. Many around me were advising me to terminate him. Bob had scheduled breakfast with me before I became CEO in an effort to head off my doubts about him. I had done nothing to reassure him that he'd remain on the team. And during the two months since, I had been watching him very closely so as to determine what to do.

I could have summarily directed Bob Frye to give RIT a response that I'd come up with. If past performance was any indication, that response would have involved giving in and adding to our ballooning deficit for fear of negative press coverage. We really didn't need to engage other members of our team. Frye and I could have worked this out on our own. But that's not how we approached this problem.

Members of our leadership team—Frye, myself, COO Steve Hendershott, and Chuck Switzer, our head of route scheduling—had running strategy discussions over a few days. We finalized the Authority's response to RIT one Thursday evening in my office. We talked for an hour. What if we took this position or that one? What were the upsides? What were the downsides? How would RIT respond? How would the media play it? Would we lay off the employees depending on how RIT responded or could we absorb them? Throughout the discussion, I didn't sit behind my desk. We gathered around the coffee table I had recently added to my office. We were addressing these issues as a team, so we met as a team.

Eventually, we decided that Frye would inform his counterpart that we would discontinue service on Route 24 when RIT's subsidy ended. My guess is that Frye and Switzer were stunned when they left my office that night. Even I wondered if we had come to the right conclusion. The Authority had never done such a thing. RIT was stunned, too. They had been convinced that we'd just keep running the route whether they funded it or not. They had forced our hand just six months earlier.

They thought we'd content ourselves with leaving at least part of a chicken in every pot, that we would do "whatever it takes." They were wrong. No check, no service, no chicken.

It took a year, but RIT wound up coming back and reinstating their subsidy. Our tough negotiating stance had led to only minimal costs for us—one day of negative coverage in the print media. Today, our business relationship with RIT is twice as large as when I started, the terms work for us, and we partner as organizations on a number of fronts. In particular, they bring extraordinary value by helping us advance our technology initiatives. Ironically enough, today it's we who send several hundred thousands of dollars *their* way. More fundamentally, though, that June night began to change things for our team. The episode emboldened us, establishing that we really were going to make key strategic decisions differently. We would debate things together and work as a team to strike deals that served our interests. We would walk away as a team when the deal didn't measure up. As I think we all realized, the debate we held was far more important than the result of the discussion. Our culture was beginning to change in ways more significant than the symbolic arrangement of chairs in my office.

"WHAT DO *YOU* THINK WE OUGHT TO DO?"

During our financial crisis, we began holding regular meetings at which all employees could learn about company policy and air their views. The Authority had previously held employee meetings once or twice a year, but these had been mainly stream-of-consciousness affairs, with different leaders telling stories, talking about interesting movies, and expounding on current events. When the subject transitioned to work, senior leaders would often sell out direct line managers in an effort to play to the crowd. The rank and file would see senior leaders as the ones with all the power, which is exactly what the leaders wanted.

In our new meetings, I still ran things, setting the tone and direction. But I didn't dominate. I only talked for the first fifteen minutes, sharing what was going on, what the key issues were, and what we were working on. Then I opened up the meeting for comments, ideas, and suggestions. I tried to engage questioners in a dialogue, asking them: "What do *you* think we ought to do?"

Of course, I had no idea what we were going to do. We hadn't yet developed a strategic plan or an operating plan to achieve the strategy. I didn't even know what a strategic or operating plan *was*! I also didn't yet know how bad the situation was, let alone how to fix it. But I did try to set the stage for what was coming.

Around 100 to 150 employees came to these early meetings. I held them every quarter because I wanted to get our people thinking in terms of quarters. Publicly traded companies report their numbers on a quarterly basis, and Wall Street reacts depending on how the results match up with expectations. I wanted us to think the same way. We were building a plan that would receive our board's public endorsement. The quarterly meetings made us all think in terms of progress toward those preestablished goals.

When it came time for employees to speak, I made sure to take notes. I would summarize at the end the things we talked about, so that employees could see I really was listening and paying attention. Some employees grandstanded. This was their chance to challenge the CEO in front of their buddies so that they could go back to their workstations and laugh about how they "showed" me. Sometimes union leadership would attend and attempt to upstage employee meetings. I made it clear that if the union wanted to hold a meeting, it could go schedule one. But this was my meeting and it would run my way. And I was interested in what the employees had to say, not some union thug who was a big reason we were in this mess to begin with.

THE BUS DOCTORS

Our broader goal was to create a culture where rank-and-file employees felt comfortable and almost obliged to say how things looked from their perspective. If an employee went home after a day's work and said something different to her spouse than what she said in a meeting, she failed that day. Looking back on it, we took it for granted that nobody worked *for* us, they worked *with* us, the paradox being that the more our people felt they worked with us, the more they wound up serving us and respecting us—in other words, working for us.

> **We took it for granted that nobody worked *for* us, they worked *with* us, the paradox being that the more our people felt they worked with us, the more they wound up serving us and respecting us—in other words, working for us.**

One way we've tried to encourage participation and a sense of ownership is by placing employees front and center in our communications. We try to send the message that the Authority is not the CEO's organization; it's all of ours. If you flip through our extensive annual Comprehensive Plan, you'll find it's inundated with pictures not of senior managers but rather of rank-and-file employees. They're whom we celebrate. And we hand the plan out to them each year, too. We also have begun putting employees in our advertising—a sharp break from the old days, when senior leaders would battle over who among them would appear in our ads. Just this past year, we began putting the names of our employees' children on the sides of our buses. We held a contest to determine who'd get the honor and hosted a weekend awards ceremony at which we unveiled the buses. Multiple generations of families came, and children got to see where their parents and grandparents worked and have their photograph taken next to a giant forty-foot bus with their name painted on the side.

Words are well and good, but we've backed up our rhetoric by also opening up the decision-making process even wider as time has passed. Bus cleanliness is a great example. Through a measurement system we built from the ground floor up, we learned we still had a problem keeping our buses clean. But instead of proclaiming from on high that drivers didn't have to drive dirty buses, we created a

Rather than spotlight executives, our advertising is built around the employees on the front line.

team of employees who went out, observed what we were doing, examined best practices across the country, and then designed a whole new process for cleaning our buses. Vice presidents didn't do it. Department heads didn't do it. No big speeches from me. A team of mid-level employees developed and implemented the process. And guess who got the credit? The employees.

BAKING COOKIES TO SHARE

In place of paternalism—and the turkey-hoarding attitude that went with it—we strove to instill a spirit of giving and service. After my first year as CEO, we gave all of our employees raises, but I quietly declined one, though our board offered it. Four years later, another opportunity arose to sacrifice on behalf of the organization, and this time the entire leadership team joined in. We had just concluded a third straight year of surpluses and had generally delivered outstanding results. We really wanted to provide raises for our employees, but we hesitated because of future financial challenges we saw looming. Our leadership team discussed the possibility of forgoing extra compensation for the coming year to see if we could be more generous with the bulk of our workforce. Every single department head agreed, feeling that this was both important and appropriate. We communicated our collective decision to the employees; that way, they could know their bosses had declined salary hikes so that they and their families could earn more.

Here's a nuance worth pondering. When I, as CEO, declined an adjustment in pay, we didn't make a big deal out of it. That would have advanced my own standing. But when our entire leadership team declined an adjustment in compensation, we pointed that out to the employees. Because now a whole team of employees had acted selflessly.

As of this writing, we've also begun to instill a no-ego culture in our physical infrastructure. We currently have a three-story Administrative Building and, 150 yards away, a large, two-story Operations Building housing our driver and dispatch areas, mechanical shops, and storage for our hundreds of buses. The physical divide creates a white collar vs. blue collar conflict that impedes our ability to think of ourselves as one family. To fill the need of our growing business for more office space, we've chosen to expand our Administrative Building not by building up, but by building across, toward the Operations Building. Our plan is to create a large post-and-beam type entry, including a covered walkway connecting the two buildings. Rather than build our first ever employee gym in either the Administration or Operations wings, we're going to build it in the connected area so that people from both groups can intermingle as equals in the gym. We're aware that this arrangement might turn off some prospective executives who might like the perk of a special gym. Our thinking is this: If a potential executive believes that he needs a nicer gym because he's a vice president—well, that's not the kind of person we want working here.

I'm happy to report that the tone of our regular celebrations has changed dramatically and for the better during my time at the Authority. We've eliminated free turkeys at the holiday parties, and as a result these occasions have ceased being grab-fests and now serve as real opportunities to embrace the holiday spirit. "I used to hear so many stories about what our parties used to be like," says Mary Anne Merrick, an executive assistant. "People grabbing everything that wasn't nailed down. Today, it's a whole different thing; we have dozens of employees who bring in Christmas cookies they baked to share with people." We also used to have an annual employee dinner for which the Authority paid for everything—all the food, open bar—and people got plastered. Now we have an annual party where people pay for their own drinks, and we even ask employees to pay a nominal fee toward the dinner's cost; there is no taking from the trough. I get up at the beginning of the dinner, thank everyone, and make some remarks commenting on the year. I hand out a few of the company-wide awards. Then I sit down, and the focus shifts to our employees. *They* hand out awards for things like driver safety and quality of customer service, and *they* announce who won our annual driver obstacle course. Usually we have an Oscars-style presentation, complete with skits and back-and-forth. It's a fun evening, and it's about our employees, not the leaders.

HOW A CULTURE OF NO EGO
ACTUALLY SAVED JOBS

It's probably impossible to demonstrate with scientific accuracy the connection between a culture of no ego and business results. Yet the connection is evident to just about anyone familiar with our turn-around. To evoke the changes we've seen in our people and the effect it's had on our business, I'd like to tell you about an important episode that took place amid the depths of our financial crisis. This is an inspiring story about a middle-level manager who had never spoken up before, yet whose contribution, because of his newfound confidence and comfort, single-handedly saved dozens of jobs.

During the first few months of my tenure, we were casting about for ways to save our company. Rather than just cut the service we put out on the street each day, we wanted to see if we could pare back routes that yielded the least amount of revenue and carried the fewest people and add service where our buses were too full. Pete MacNaughton, a manager in our Dispatch Center and a regular at the team meetings, was tasked with putting buses where people wanted to go, when they wanted to go there. I insisted that he participate on the team because he was one of those closest to the action. I didn't want these decisions made just by people with ties. With twenty-two years of experience, MacNaughton held a wealth of knowledge. He had been a bus driver for years before being promoted to dispatcher, so he knew the intricacies of the Authority's biggest annual expense: sending RGRTA buses out on the street. Yet he had never been asked for input.

We had already identified about 12 percent of the buses we scheduled every day as significant underperformers. Those 12 percent were picking up either very few people or, in many cases, absolutely nobody. So our working group gathered and talked our way through what it would mean to operate this service more smartly. Questions we considered included how to go about implementing the changes, what they would mean for employees and customers, and how to notify the public.

At our first meeting, several people were in the room. Chuck Switzer and a couple of his teammates in the Scheduling Department. Debbie Griffith from Human Resources. Retired Rochester police captain Bruce Philpott, our director of operations who oversaw all of our bus drivers. Steve Hendershott and Bob Frye. MacNaughton sat very quietly and did a lot of listening. It was clear we were going to need fewer employees. The conclusions from Finance indicated we could do with about thirty fewer bus drivers and seven fewer mechanics. Pete has a beard, yet you could almost see the tension in his jaw as he looked through glasses thick from reading bus schedules for so many years. He was scared out of his wits. Like many other mid-level employees, his ears still rang with rantings he used to hear about firing all of the road supervisors, radio controllers, and dispatchers. It was no easy thing for him to sit down in our boardroom with the new CEO, the COO, the CFO, the director of labor relations, and the vice president of scheduling to talk about possible layoffs.

With short blond hair, Debbie was sitting just to my left. Her office was in the Operations Building, so she had regular interaction with MacNaughton. He understandably chose to sit next to her.

Bob Frye sat across the table from all of us. And he was anxious to cut the routes. He wanted to see the financial results that would accrue from sending out fewer paychecks, buying less fuel, and ordering fewer buses. He had called the shots around there for a long time, and for him, saving money had always been the purpose. I wanted to save money, too, but more fundamentally I wanted to improve efficiency. We'd designed our new process not to save money, but to drive higher productivity. Saving money was the result, not the purpose. What Bob didn't see—and what I wondered if he could ever see—was that layoffs weren't an automatic win for us, since they would demoralize our workforce and reduce its productivity. They also ran the risk of causing public relations problems. If you've ever laid off unionized public employees, or read about it in the newspaper, you know that they don't just say thank you for the opportunity and go find work elsewhere. They complain. Loudly. And the media loves it.

Saving money was the result, not the purpose.

We pored over data, trying to figure out if there might be another way to reduce the workforce without laying employees off. From the first, we had taken as our goal solving the economic crisis while still keeping fares stable for our customers and feeding the 750 families who depended on us for paychecks. That responsibility weighed on all of us, including Frye. It certainly weighed very heavily on me. I bite my cuticles when I am under pressure, and with

36

all of the financial challenges the organization was facing, and now with the prospect of major changes in service that might reduce our workforce, my fingers were raw and bleeding. I started to cover them in Band-Aids just so I couldn't get at them.

Frye dominated the discussion. Citing budgeting formulas he had long used, he argued passionately about how many employees we should lay off and how we should go about doing it. "We can sit here with all the fancy formulas we want. But at the end of the day, we need fewer people, and the longer we dillydally, the more people we're going to have to get rid of." I kept thinking about what the layoffs would mean to the families of those employees. How they would demoralize the workforce. And balancing that against the fact that our remaining funds would run out before year's end. We concluded the first meeting by sending people back to gather more information. And once again, I found myself wondering how much longer it would make sense to keep Bob around.

I'm sure Frye and others thought I was being indecisive as we all got up and exited the boardroom. All this work. All this analysis. All this talk about finding a new way to do business and promote culture change. And now I wouldn't have the stomach for it. I was going to be just like every other public sector so-called leader with a fancy title. But they could think what they wanted; I wasn't going to be forced into this. The result of our change in thought process didn't have to be the traditional conclusion.

By the next meeting, MacNaughton was starting to find his sea legs. As folks began to file in, he chose to sit this time on the other side of the table, away from Debbie. He could see that our decision-making process was different from that which had existed for so many years. We really did want him engaged. His job wasn't in jeopardy if he said something contrary to what we were all thinking. For the first time in his career at the Authority, MacNaughton could have an impact on policy and, in this case, affect dozens of lives. I asked him lots of questions. I was very careful with my tone and the phrasing, trying to draw him in, as I knew he could help us. We just needed him to see that the CEO's presence didn't automatically mean his job was at stake.

After some discussion, it became clear that we were paying exorbitant levels of overtime pay. This practice had been going on for years, and it had always been considered the price of doing business. MacNaughton took a risk, wading in with an idea for using our drivers more strategically and reducing the amount of overtime that we were paying. "Look," he said, his voice wavering. "Every single morning at 4 A.M., we are on the phone in Dispatch trying to get extra drivers to come in because of all the people that have called in sick or just don't even bother showing up. And because of that we have drivers who are purposely not driving their regular routes, because they know they're going to get called for overtime. For years now, there are drivers who will work forty hours of straight time and then forty hours of overtime on top of that. Routinely they do that."

The white collar people in the room sat quietly. You could see jaws dropping. We didn't do the payroll. How would we know about this stuff? But MacNaughton did. That's what he did every day. "If we can grow the number of drivers that I have available in the morning," MacNaughton said, "and if we can be more flexible with not having to call people in, attendance will improve, and overtime will drop like a rock."

We went back and forth, critiquing MacNaughton's idea, taking it apart, analyzing the possible effects of changing up our scheduling. Frye in particular attacked MacNaughton's argument. But Pete had come to play. He had the actual call sheets that he had worked off just that morning and could show how we paid more than two hundred hours in overtime just that day because of drivers who had simply not shown up. "You're missing the point," he said, standing toe to toe with Frye. "They know they don't have to come in. Because they'll be able to make up this time easily at a different point in the week. Only then they'll be doing it at time and a half."

I can only imagine how exhausted MacNaughton must have felt later that day upon leaving the boardroom. I don't know if he came expecting to participate and offer up that suggestion, or if the uninformed opinions around the table frustrated him and caused him to speak. As we all got up, I darted around the table to catch him before he left. I really wanted to thank him for engaging. I'm sure he felt some level of exposure for having argued with our CFO, and I wanted to assure him that we appreciated his candor. I think he left that day feeling like he was having an impact way beyond anything he had ever done on the job.

We held three more sessions to analyze the effects of Mac-Naughton's proposed scheduling change. In the end, we were divided between two choices: lay off dozens of bus drivers and continue to protect the massive overtime pay that many drivers were taking advantage of; or enact the MacNaughton plan, whereby we would drastically alter our business practice and eliminate most overtime, but keep all employees working. Frye remained very strong in arguing that we had to lay off some drivers and mechanics to reduce head count, that it was the only way we were going to save money. Our vice president of scheduling, Chuck Switzer, backed him up. Based on how he was scheduling the work, he felt that we simply didn't need that many drivers.

I wasn't sure what to do. This was a huge decision, and I had two seasoned executives in open disagreement with someone who had no leadership credentials. I wrestled with this question for two days before deciding. We would go with MacNaughton's plan, cutting back on overtime and meeting our financial goals, but saving dozens of jobs. I can't emphasize enough how important Pete's contribution was and how personally invested he became in the process, at great perceived risk to himself. At one point during the approximately sixty days of analysis that we gave to this project, MacNaughton was scheduled to go on vacation. He was so interested in the discussion, and he believed so much in the solution he had designed, that he came in for one of our team meetings and left his wife sitting in the parking lot for three hours so that they could continue on vacation after the meeting. Talk about a motivated employee. That is success, on a lot of levels. That's the culture of no ego.

About six months later, after we had navigated through the worst of our financial crisis, we held our annual Employee Recognition Awards event, recognizing our employees for work they had done the previous year. We handed out awards for safety, for perfect attendance, and for going above and beyond the call of duty. Employees were nominated by their department head for these awards, and a committee determined whom we would honor. Surprisingly enough, Pete MacNaughton had not been nominated by his supervisor for an award. I spotted this oversight and nominated him myself.

The day of the Employee Recognition event, I learned that Pete wasn't going to attend because he didn't want to be teased by the drivers for having won an award. I called over to the dispatch office. In all his twenty-two years, he had probably never received a phone call directly from the CEO. "Look, Pete," I said, "you don't have to come if you don't want to. I'm certainly not going to make you. But I really would like you to come. You saved these people's jobs. You know it. I know it. And it helps me to send a very strong message to people here that their job is not an entitlement, and that our organization isn't a gravy train. That we don't exist just to hand out money every week. I would really appreciate it if you would consider coming."

"Okay," he replied. "If you want me to come, I'd be happy to."

At our recognition event, I proudly gave eight employees our "Above and Beyond" award for going beyond the call of duty. And I told the several hundred employees gathered that if they were one of the thirty least senior bus drivers and one of the seven least senior mechanics, then they should make a point of thanking Pete Mac-Naughton for the fact that they still worked here. He had saved their jobs. Pete was embarrassed. And he was beaming, too. He took some teasing. And I watched some people personally thank him. He had gone way above and beyond. He symbolized our new management approach of changing the culture so that people four levels down on the organizational chart not only challenged senior management, but felt motivated and inspired to do their very best for the good of all, even if this meant putting their own necks on the line.

"IT HAS NOTHING TO DO WITH ME"

My talk about participatory decision-making and community spirit among employees might sound idealistic to some of you more hard-nosed readers. Yet something intangible like culture does have perceptible results. Look around our company today, and you'll find an abundance of energy, enthusiasm, passion, and creativity. People here care about each other, whether it's our Sunshine Committee, which performs acts of kindness when employees experience personal tragedies, or our innovative wellness program, which a committee of employees created on their own initiative. Although every organization has its bad apples, employees here really do go the extra mile, in most cases without expecting special recognition or rewards.

A great example is Millie Rosa, a veteran employee in her early thirties. All day long she works in our call center, taking customer complaints and information requests. In 2008, an employee committee evaluated her work using a quantitative scoring method and nominated her for the American Public Transportation Association's first ever award for the country's best call center agent. Millie represented our company at the national competition in Disney World— and she won! We made a huge deal of this, bringing her in front of our board and the media, since her victory validated all the work we'd done to get people to think of "customers" instead of "passengers." Call center employees seldom receive recognition, and this was Millie's big chance. Yet at every single event, Millie never spoke of "I" or "me," but rather what "*we* do as an organization." She would make sure to note: "Any one of my colleagues would have won the competition as well, that's how we operate as a team and as an organization, this is how we do things—it has nothing to do with me, but how we operate."

Over the past five years, we've seen even hardened employees come around and get behind the organization. In 2006, New York State governor George Pataki announced that our transit system would receive an equitable portion of state aid. Not a bailout, but equity. Everyone had worked so hard for two years to turn our organization around. To celebrate what truly was a collective milestone, we held an elaborate, pep rally–style event with hundreds of our employees in one of our massive bus garages. I announced that all employees would have a chance to sign the Comprehensive Plan we were submitting to our board. Previously, it had only been signed by the CEO and the CFO. "If you feel like you helped this year," I said, "if you feel you got out in front of the wagon and pulled to get us through the mud when we were stuck, then I want you to sign the letter."

With balloons still falling, U2's "Beautiful Day" still playing, and our employees congratulating one another and milling about, Caesar McFadden made his way over to me. "Look, I'm not signing the letter."

"Here we go," I thought. There was no way a guy like McFadden was going to bring me down on a day like this. "That's okay, Caesar," I said. "It's totally up to you."

"But let me tell you why," he said, interrupting. "I'm not gonna sign the letter because I can't."

For a second I wondered if Caesar didn't have the ability to read or write. Sadly, some of our employees don't.

"I'm not going to sign the letter," he continued, "because I didn't believe. I was a disruption. I was embarrassing. I didn't help move us forward. I took shots. I sat in the back and watched." He opened his eyes wide, looking right at me. "I don't deserve to sign the letter. But next year—next year, that's gonna change. I will believe. I will honor what we do. I will help."

It was a fantastic moment. Here was a formerly antagonistic employee looking inward and openly admitting his flaws. He had transcended ego, just like our organization as a whole had, and we all were better off for it.

We've come a long way from the free hot dog stand and friends of employees walking out with aluminum foil–covered plates of bar-bequed ribs. That culture of "me first" had created an attitude of "customer last"—and had bled our bottom line dry.

Our problems were so big, and they so threatened our ability to survive, that we needed to focus on something foundational—culture—in order to improve our bottom line. When you're broke, it usually makes sense to focus first on money. We were *so* broke we focused on minds.

And with our employees' minds now fully engaged, we were poised to take full advantage.

2.

THE MARKETPLACE IS BIGGER THAN YOUR BUS

Listening Means More Than Just to Customers

I held my first news conference about a month after becoming CEO. I was nervous. *Really* nervous. I had organized hundreds of news events before, while working as a staff member for a congressman, but I had never been the one standing behind the podium. What really put me on edge was what I was about to say. I was introducing a major initiative, one that might seem strange for a bus company: We were going to stop picking up passengers.

That would certainly make some news. A public transportation system that no longer picked up passengers. How could a bus company stop picking up passengers?

Simple. We were going to start picking up customers.

Our director of communications had done a terrific job of creating visual props for the TV cameras and convincing the media that we had a major announcement. All the news media turned out that day—five TV stations, the local newspaper, and two radio stations. As I rode the elevator down to our first-floor boardroom, I could feel my heart pounding. I stepped up to the podium, our county executive, Maggie Brooks, by my side. Behind me, formal blue draperies flowed to the floor. An American flag hung on a pole to my left, a

New York State flag to my right. The room felt tiny, and it seemed like a thousand lights were pointed at me. My mouth was parched as I began to describe our decision to unveil Driving Excellence, our new customer service campaign.

For as long as anyone could remember, our company had viewed users of our service as passive beings who didn't exercise choice and who used our service as a manner of course. As a result, our own employees embraced an attitude of "take it or leave it." It didn't matter if the bus was on time, or if it was clean, or if the driver was polite. Take it or leave it—what other choice would a passenger have?

Not that this attitude was unique to us. It's epidemic in public transportation and throughout government. Do the public schools in your town strike you as dedicated to excellence? How about your Department of Motor Vehicles, with its unhelpful civil servants standing behind the counter? In the private sector, it drives me crazy when I hear a flight attendant ask all passengers to return to their seats. "I'm not a passenger," I think to myself. "I paid for this seat. I'm a customer." Likewise, newspapers typically serve subscribers, and television stations viewers, not customers. Maybe that's why so few enjoy strong customer loyalty.

We had to do better. In order to stabilize our long-term financial future, we needed to develop a product that people—*customers*— would choose to buy. We'd improve bus cleanliness, revamp our bus stop signs to make them more informative, sell bus passes on our website, deploy technology that allowed customers to know when the next bus would arrive—and that was just the beginning. Although many of our customers were poor, we wouldn't take them for granted. In the years to come, we'd show them a product worth buying.

I didn't do so well that day as a communicator. Dazzled by the flashbulbs and the bright lights of the television cameras, I rushed through the material. I read way too much from my notes, rather than speaking from my heart. My voice wavered. I judged it a solid four out of ten.

Our communications person ducked her head into my office just after the news conference and flashed me a thumbs-up, but I knew better. I had watched too many of these events from the other side of the podium.

Fortunately, my own performance didn't matter so much. What mattered was that we were devoting an entire news conference, our first, to the theme of serving customers. I didn't expect that people in the public would remember or even notice what I was saying, but I sure did hope our employees would. If we were to give our customers a real choice, our employees would need to revolutionize the way they went about their daily work. Just as important, they would have to put their ears to the ground and listen to customers on our behalf. We couldn't serve our customers if we didn't know who these people were and what they wanted.

Large corporations do many things to learn about markets. Mostly they focus on developing customers as their information source. They run focus groups, put out quantitative surveys, and watch how people behave in their homes. Our company had done market research sporadically, but we didn't have a formal structure for understanding and tracking customer attitudes. We would have to design, build, and implement that, but before we did, we made a strategic decision to start gathering information from a source few people think to tap: the very employees who interacted with customers on a daily basis.

PIPE BOMBS AND PISSING CONTESTS

I expect some of you will greet this decision with skepticism. Some of you might have written off your own cashiers, drivers, or hotel maids as an unlikely and unreliable source of insight into customers. "They're limited," so many managers think. "They don't know what they're talking about. It's just too hard to understand them, and the payback is so paltry."

Our own senior managers once thought like that. Some of them even discouraged me from paying more attention to the ideas of front-line employees. These managers had worked their way up in the organization, had nicer chairs, and they felt that they were more knowledgeable than people like Pete MacNaughton, whom they considered their subordinates. As I said to these managers, we had no choice. We were failing if we had a bunch of people in white shirts and ties sitting around a conference room table making decisions about our customers. We needed to engage and involve those people in our workforce who interacted with our customers most directly and who understood their needs and desires intimately.

When I played JV basketball, the coach once sat all seventeen of us teammates down along the baseline underneath the basket and asked where on the court we felt most confident we could score. It was a Sunday morning practice at Mayfield High School. We got up one by one with a basketball and showed our teammates where our sweet spot was. In business, you also put your teammates in the position where you can best take advantage of their talents. You don't ask the bus driver how to enter into a fixed market swap for fuel prices, or how to put together a multi-year financial plan. By the same token, you don't ask the CFO how to improve the frequency of bus service to the Wal-Mart on Hudson Avenue, or what people in a certain inner-city neighborhood think about the schedule. You ask the front-line crew.

Managers often suspect their employees are too disengaged or disgruntled to volunteer quality information. Maybe they fear employees will purposely sabotage the organization by giving false information. Let me ask: Do your employees write on walls with their own feces? Do they come to work high on marijuana and shout at the customers? Do they fight with one another and have sex on buses? Do they hurl racial epithets at some of your customers? Our employees have done all these things—and then some. But that didn't stop us from trying to secure their cooperation, even before our culture of no ego took hold. And it didn't stop us from gaining valuable insights into our market as a result.

Let me give you a better sense of how tough and uncooperative our workforce was and, to some extent, continues to be. Our organization has suffered decades of severe labor-relations problems. We've had shouting matches, strikes, work slowdowns, attendance issues, and small acts of sabotage. Tensions have even given way to outright violence. During the early 1990s, the Authority tried to alter work times so that maintenance employees would put in more night hours, when most buses were in the garage. Maintenance staff didn't like the idea very much, so some of them went into the office area where senior operations managers worked and set off a pipe bomb in the middle of a workday.* Nobody was hurt, and our organization opted (mistakenly, I believe) not to call the police or publicize the incident. Our leadership also quietly backed down from the proposed changes. "It was unbelievable," Rich Kirtland, one of our garage foremen remembers. "It was a pretty big boom. Could have killed somebody. I felt like a prison riot was about to break out."

Another notorious incident took place soon after I became CEO, when we renovated our quiet room. A number of our drivers work split shifts, driving in the morning and later in the day. Some go home or run errands, some stick around and shoot pool or play cards in the active drivers' room, but some just want to retire into a quiet space to read or rest. We had invested in nice, comfortable furniture for the room, but a week or two before we reopened it, an employee went in and urinated all over the new furniture. We tried to find out who did it, but nobody would rat on the culprit, and of course, nobody confessed. We closed the quiet room and informed our employees that it would stay closed until we either learned the identities of the perpetrators or the union leadership agreed to pay

---

*At least we think it was a pipe bomb. It might have been another kind of explosive, such as a stick of dynamite.

for damages if another act of vandalism occurred. As of this writing, the quiet room remains closed, even though drivers ask me all the time to forget about what happened and reopen it.

And then there's our 2008 bus rodeo. In this annual event, our drivers compete in an elaborate obstacle course. The top three finishers represent our company at the state level, and the winner of that competition goes on to compete for fame and fortune at the national rodeo. Our employees have won both the state and national competitions. It's really exciting for our company and even our community.

The union leadership somehow thinks this rodeo is for management rather than the employees, even though our administrative employees volunteer their time on a Saturday to man the obstacles. In 2008, our union employees were still working without a contract after two years of negotiations. When rodeo time came around, union leadership decided to picket the event. They had threatened this before, and management had typically responded by canceling the rodeo—something that had only empowered the union leadership. Well, times were different now. We held firm, proclaiming that if even one driver wanted to drive, we would hold a rodeo. Typically, fifty drivers participate. That year, six showed, and they had to cross a picket line of their colleagues holding signs and bullhorns. These were people they'd have to see the next day at work.

We had upped the ante: For the first time in decades, we would hold our Employee Recognition dinner the same night as the bus rodeo, to announce the winners along with recipients of other awards. The picket line that night at the employee dinner was especially loud, aggressive, and mean-spirited. When I arrived at the suburban hotel where we were holding the event, there were probably seventy protesters screaming and chanting insults. Then the six union employees who'd participated in our rodeo arrived. A handful of others who hadn't participated came, too. Some brought their wives, and they had to drive straight through the picket line. If the picketers had greeted me harshly, they treated these employees even worse, pounding on their car windshields, pointing, and shouting at the tops of their lungs. One of the employees' wives, a first-generation Eastern European immigrant, was really shaken. During the dinner, I thanked these employees for being so courageous. They said they had been hell-bent on coming. "Of course I'm glad I came," said the man whose wife had been shaken up. "There was no way I was going to let anybody stop us from doing what I thought was right."

DRIVING UNDER THE FLAG

As managers, we can't simply proclaim our intent to listen to employees; we have to set up new institutions within the organization. That way, employees realize these activities are here to stay, and they feel more comfortable contributing. They overcome their sense that it is not their "place" to put forth ideas and that "nobody's listening anyway." One of the first things we did was spotlight a special advisory group I'd created made up almost exclusively of drivers and our customer service representatives. Only two members of the leadership team participated in the group, myself and Ann Nichols, our director of customer service. We wanted front-line employees dominating the room, not managers. Meeting quarterly, this team was charged with conceiving new initiatives to improve customer experience and to help our employees deliver that improved experience. We named this group FLAG, or the Front-Line Advisory Group.

One hope I had in establishing FLAG was to bypass union leadership and communicate directly with our drivers. I wanted a chance to learn how things were going both operationally and for our customers. Further, if these employees had been offering suggestions and concerns to their supervisors but having them neglected, this group would allow me to try to solve some of their problems and also to establish better policies based on what was actually happening.

Our meetings took place in our customer call center instead of in my office. We established a simple set of rules. We would use our allotted time to keep track of people's suggestions and thoughts, and in between meetings we would perform research to validate these thoughts and push them on the path toward becoming full-fledged initiatives. The first agenda item for the next meeting was reporting our conclusions about the past meeting's suggestions. With meetings structured in this way, front-line employees could see which of their suggestions had been implemented, which had not, and why. They understood that this wasn't just a happy-talk group, but rather a gathering where the issues they raised would be met with answers at the following meeting. We wouldn't always do what they wanted, but they would always get an answer and an explanation. And hopefully, talk of this positive experience would filter outward into the organization, encouraging other front-line employees to volunteer new ideas to managers in other forums.

Over the first few years of this group's existence, employees came up with a number of helpful suggestions. Over at a local high school, kids had to cross a very busy street in order to board our buses because of where the bus stop was located. With input from our FLAG employees, we relocated the bus stop sign so students wouldn't have to cross the road. Very small issue. Yet we wouldn't have known about it if it weren't for FLAG. In another instance, our buses were getting bogged down because the route they were driving had them pulling into a Wal-Mart parking lot and then exiting onto a busy street at a different location that lacked a traffic light. Our scheduling staff, the people who set the routes up for our buses, didn't go out and drive the buses every day, and so they had no way of knowing that this problem existed. All they knew was that buses on the route that served the Wal-Mart store were consistently late, inconveniencing our customers. The drivers on our FLAG team knew why this was, and they also knew that customers wouldn't care much if the bus exited at a different point, near a traffic light. With the FLAG team's help, we rerouted the bus to avoid this problem, improving customer service.

When I think about the many ways we now serve customers better because of suggestions from our FLAG employees, it is very satisfying. Our buses now offer service to a Wal-Mart in one local town on Sundays—something customers wanted, but that we didn't do before. We staff a booth with a customer service coordinator at our downtown hub, to pass on route information and advice to customers. This employee works right on the street, interacting with customers to improve their experience. We also altered our summer pass program, making passes valid all day to eliminate confusion and conflict. We changed our procedures so that customers didn't have to announce to drivers that they were purchasing an all-day pass before inserting money into the fare box—an annoying step that had been required before. These are little improvements that alone wouldn't have impacted our organizational performance. Taken together, they contributed mightily toward our goal of giving people a transportation option they *wanted* to buy. So much for the idea that a hostile workforce can't contribute to consumer knowledge, or that consulting with employees isn't worth managers' time.

MAKING OUR FARE FAIR

The single greatest contribution the FLAG group has made concerned the revamping of our entire fare structure. I'd like to spend a little time telling this story, not only because the fare structure is a defining feature of every company in our industry, but because this story dramatizes so well how much more customer focused we became by consulting our front-line employees.

In 2005, we looked in-depth at how we could modernize the fares we charged our customers. Based on what you've read so far, you probably wouldn't be so surprised to learn that our existing fare structure dated from the 1960s. In typical government fashion, previous leaders had recognized the inadequacy of this structure, but they hadn't done what it took to effect change. Sure, they per-

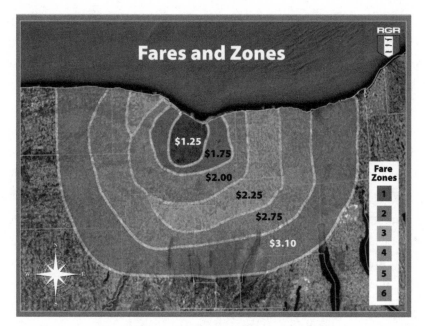

RGRTA's fare structure when I became CEO.

formed studies on the issue. But studies for the sake of wasting more time. Meanwhile, our community had changed. The population of the urban core had dropped by 35 percent over those decades, while the number of jobs in the urban core had dropped by almost 20 percent. We now felt determined to catch up to these changes. "We were getting phone calls all the time," customer service rep Millie Rosa remembers. "People frustrated by our fare system. They needed to go to jobs ten miles outside of town, and it was costing people too much to get there. All we felt we could do was just explain to people how it worked. Never even occurred to us we could change it."

The old structure was built around a zone system, which made sense thirty-five years ago when a lot of people worked in downtown Rochester. Businesses were locating there and shopping was plentiful. That people wanted to go there was reflected in our fare structure. The farther outside the city you lived, the higher the price you paid to ride the bus to get into the city. We divided our area into six concentric rings surrounding the urban core. Each time you passed over one of those invisible rings, whether heading into the city or out, the price to ride the bus became higher.

Digging a little deeper, we can appreciate how unhelpful this fare structure was in 2010. As a consequence of our system, about half the people who rode the bus in Rochester had to change buses to arrive at their ultimate destination. Think of when you fly. If you want to fly from Richmond, Virginia, to St. Louis, Missouri, chances are that you're going to transfer somewhere along the way to get there. Riding the bus in Rochester, or most communities for that matter, was exactly the same. Except that unlike the flight from Richmond to St. Louis, we charged you to transfer. That's what most public transportation systems across the United States do. Yet it's extraordinarily unfriendly to customers. If Jet Blue started doing this, customers wouldn't stand for it. Congress would have hearings. They might even do a study!

It was even worse for us. Under our six-zone system with transfers, if you lived in the city of Rochester, as most of our customers did, you could board the bus in Zone 1 and pay the driver a fare. You'd get off the bus downtown and pay the driver a second time, requesting a transfer to another route. You'd then get on to your second bus and ride out to your job in the suburbs, where so many of the jobs had gone, but because your bus had crossed one of those invisible concentric rings into another zone, you had to now give the driver more money before he'd let you get off the bus.

The transfer situation caused other, very serious problems. First, customers were abusing the system. A transfer cost fifteen cents. But once customers purchased a transfer on their first bus for that price, we had no way of tracking its use. People would buy a transfer, get off their bus downtown, and then sell their transfer for fifty or seventy-five cents to someone waiting for a bus, since the base fare to ride the bus just in Zone 1 was $1.25. If the sale price was seventy-five cents, the seller just made sixty cents. And the person who bought the transfer for seventy-five cents just saved fifty cents, because he no longer had to pay us $1.25; he could just "pretend" that he was the original transferring customer. Meanwhile, our organization lost $1.25. "I can't tell you how often people did that," driver Jim Peasley says. "I don't know how much we lost, but I bet I could retire off it."

The transfer process also invited hostility between drivers and customers. A transfer was good for two hours. That meant from the time the customer purchased it from the driver, he or she had two hours to change buses and get on board the second bus. If the original bus ran late, or if the second bus had broken down or got stuck in traffic, the time could get tight, leading customers to become frustrated. We heard about drivers stabbed, kicked, punched, and literally beaten by a mob over a simple fifteen-cent transfer. "I'll always remember some punk kid spitting on me," FLAG driver Roland Melvin says. "Over fifteen goddamn cents. That's why I brought the episode up in the meeting."

These problems with transfers were bad, but there was a more fundamental problem: Our existing fare structure was patently unfair. The structure required suburban customers to pay more to get downtown the farther out they lived—something that made sense years before, when downtown was a shopping and employment destination. Today, more affluent suburban riders didn't need to get downtown. Rather, poorer city residents, the bulk of our current customer base, needed to get to suburbia. That was where the job growth was. And the cool retail stores. And the vocational schools and community colleges. While our six-zone fare structure was supposedly charging suburban customers a premium fare to get to downtown Rochester, in truth it was charging our city customers more to get to the suburbs for work, shopping, and school.

The most visible example of this was on Route 24, which had played a role in our contract dispute with the Rochester Institute of

Technology. This line ran from the city out to Marketplace Mall in the suburb of Henrietta, before continuing on to RIT. Every single day, and particularly on the weekends, hundreds of our customers would get off the bus at the intersection of West Henrietta Road and Brighton-Henrietta Town Line Road. These customers would then walk half a mile along the very busy West Henrietta Road to the mall, without lights, without sidewalks, even though the bus would have dropped them off right at the mall's front door. I lived in this part of town for years and used to watch dozens of people huddled in a shelter at this intersection. I never understood it. There wasn't a lot going on around this stop. It turned out that when they got off the bus at Marketplace Mall, the driver would charge them an extra fifty cents for traveling into another zone. This stop stood at the invisible boundary between zones on our map. Our customers took their lives into their hands because of our outdated fare structure. So much for charging suburban customers more. The people we were hurting were city residents—just trying to get to their low-paying service jobs.

Now, guess who alerted us to the litany of problems that our old fare structure created? Guess who advocated for change month after month while our redesign process was taking place? Members of our FLAG team. Our bus drivers. The front-line guys. People like Roland Melvin, who had spent decades driving for us. Or Bruce Mackin, a heavyset fast talker with thinning black hair. Both of these guys felt so passionately about these issues that Ann Nichols and I found ourselves wanting to listen even harder. Sometimes I would ask Roland and Bruce to repeat their points two or three times so I could fully understand them.

"We really enjoyed this whole FLAG thing," Bruce Mackin tells me. "I used to be excited coming to work if we had a meeting going on that day. It felt like we were making a real difference." Tim Quinlan, one of our radio controllers, agrees. "Our whole fare system was a disaster. I don't think many people at the top really understood for a long time. But all of a sudden, we got to sit down and talk to the bosses. At first, I wasn't sure if we weren't just spinning our wheels. But they listened."

Over time, our collective experience working with fare restructuring had an important side benefit: chipping away at the authority of our unhelpful union leaders. Whereas drivers used to go to their union leadership with ideas, leaving it to the union to approach operations staff (who might or might not act on the suggestion), now rank-and-file drivers started going to FLAG team members with their ideas because they realized that they had direct access to the CEO. FLAG team members had been going back to their fellow drivers, telling them about this new venue where things were actually getting done, and word had spread that if you wanted to see something change you should talk to a FLAG member. Drivers began to research whether lifts worked for wheelchair customers, how best to improve on-time performance on a particular route, whether microphones worked to announce stops for visually impaired customers. For us, this was really exciting stuff!

In response to employee feedback, we initiated our own study—a serious one this time. The employees had given us ideas as to how to proceed; they got us to focus on the issue and understand it as never before. But this was a huge deal. You don't just make monumental changes based on an employee group. We hired consultants who came up with models reflecting all kinds of things that transit companies were doing across the country. In evaluating these models over a period of months, our priorities shifted. Initially, we were staring at a massive operating deficit and needed more revenue to keep operations afloat, so this priority reigned over customer service. Later, though, as our financial position strengthened, and as so many of the initiatives we were enacting took hold and had an impact, we came to see it as more important to build a customer-friendly fare structure. We began to transition our thinking to a new fare structure that didn't increase our revenues, but that made the fares we charged fairer for our current customers, easier to understand for new customers, and less likely to produce conflict between employees and customers. This, we thought, would be the smart play.

What if we completely eliminated the price of transfers and incorporated it into the price? What if we made all the zones go away and just charged everyone the same price? When you fly or take a train, you pay once. You give the company money, they take you where you want to go. Period. What if we did exactly that? No more invisible zones where the drivers made you hand over more money before they let you get off the bus. As members of our FLAG team confirmed, this change would reflect our community's evolving demography. With no more zones, our city customers could now get to the suburbs for less. As I recall, Bob Frye liked this idea when it was proposed. "Let's get the structure as strong as it can be," he said. "We can worry about the price later." "Did I hear that right?" I remember thinking. "Bob Frye, the old-guard finance guy, putting customer experience ahead of money?"

That took care of one set of problems. Yet we couldn't just eliminate transfers with our new concept of one price all the time for everybody. The honest customers who were transferring properly were paying just fifteen cents for their second ride to complete their journey. If we eliminated transfers altogether, they would pay appreciably more. So we added the concept of a day pass. A customer could purchase a pass right on the bus good for unlimited rides all day long, anywhere they wanted to go. No transfers. No time limits. No zones. Problem solved. One price for everybody, anywhere.

Thanks to our front-line employees, we had arrived at the system that we wanted. And in keeping with our efforts to engage employees, we announced the new structure to them before anyone else at our March 2006 employee meeting. I still smile when I think of one of the questions I handled that day. Frank Falzone, one of the elected union officials, a heavy man whose shirt couldn't button all the way to the top, raised his hand, seeking to challenge me. He was standing in the back of the meeting, arms folded, amid a group of mechanics and drivers. "So you're just eliminating transfers," he said in a menacing tone.

Our new, simplified fare structure, created through employee feedback,
drove customer satisfaction up substantially.

"That's right," I said. "Gone."

His expression changed, his eyes softening. "That's good. That's very good. Long overdue." And then he started a round of applause.

I couldn't believe what I was seeing. If the pope had walked in, I doubt I would have been more surprised. FLAG had won.

Not long after this meeting, we made our new fare structure public. The community was poised for us to raise fares because our organization hadn't raised them in eleven years and the price of gas had dominated the news for the past year. We announced that our new fare to ride any RTS bus anywhere you wanted to go would be what our lowest price was at that time, $1.25. And if you changed buses, as many did in our system, you could purchase an all day Freedom Pass for $3.00. For just $3.00 you could ride all day long, anywhere you wanted to go, as many times as you wanted, and take as long as you wanted to transfer.

One young woman, a receptionist at a local hotel, pulled me aside. "I just wanted to tell you that I ride your bus every day from my apartment out to SUNY Brockport [the State University at Brockport], where I'm taking classes. And then I ride the bus back in and work here at the hotel all night. Your idea to change the fare is going to save me seven dollars every day. Thank you for doing it." I wish she could have thanked the FLAG folks. They're the ones who deserved it.

The entire week before the new structure went into effect, a large team of our employees spent ten hours a day down on Main Street, riding the buses and approaching customers, handing out information so that people would understand it. It was clear after a couple of days that the public was understanding it. And they were liking it. Debbie Griffith, our former director of labor relations who a year earlier had been promoted to vice president of human resources, was very excited. "We're really resonating with people," she said. "I'm just having a great time being out here. I get the feeling that this change will really help folks."

Her impressions were later borne out by a performance measurement system we had introduced, called our Customer Satisfaction Index. We had used it for the first time the quarter before. After the fare restructuring, our numbers skyrocketed. As a result of the simplified system, ease of paying the fare shot up 27 percent. Ease of purchasing fare media went up 26 percent. As Ann Nichols recalls, "These were huge favorable bumps. We had just started to measure customer satisfaction, and here we were seeing really clear proof that we had gotten this new fare structure, well, fair." This was also clear proof that listening to line employees could make a big difference in how we understood and served our market. "We just knew this would work," Roland Melvin says. "When you're doing the same thing over and over again every single day, you learn stuff. Guys around the building talk about stuff all the time. But the thing is, we're just bitching to each other. People up top have got to listen to us. I'm really glad about the FLAG meetings because now we do get heard. The company does things better for us and also better for people on the buses. I see the results every day."

TRIP SCORING

Employees' operational suggestions so often are valuable, sometimes even pivotal. Our urban population has declined by about 5 percent over the past eight years, yet our ridership has *increased* more than 20 percent as compared to five years ago, dramatically higher than the national average. We wouldn't have been able to post numbers like that without the great operational thinking of our rank-and-file and mid-level workforce. The best example I can think of has to do with the creation of our innovative, industry-leading system for evaluating the productivity of individual trips our buses take, what we call "Trip Scoring."

In 2004, when we were facing our financial crisis, we didn't just think about cutting expenses or boosting revenue. The board had been presented with a budget that wouldn't get us through the current year. We'd be out of money and still have weeks to go. We asked, "Is there a way to deliver a product that people want to buy in a more efficient and effective fashion? How might we alter our schedules so as to increase the number of people who ride the average bus—in other words, to arrive at more productive routes?" To answer these questions, we convened a series of off-site meetings involving members of our leadership team.

At the first meeting, I could sense that people had not bought into the need to make our routes more productive and efficient. I was probably sensitive to this, given a recent altercation I'd had with one especially important person in the room, Bob Frye. Despite the broader thinking he'd shown during our fare restructuring meetings, I still hadn't decided whether I would keep Bob on as our CFO. Just the other day, I'd learned that he was trying to micromanage our

Parts Department, which didn't report to him. I was furious, and we'd had it out.

We'd calmed down a bit since, but tension between us still ran deep. Now, sitting in a meeting with him and other executives, I was

I saw the financial benefits as the *result* of a new scheduling process, not as the objective.

determined to stand strong with him as far as my ideas about efficiency were concerned. Unlike Bob and some others, I didn't want service cuts for their own sake.

That was the typical transit model. You were cutting just to save money. You weren't altering the business model. We'd be right back the next year cutting more service. I wanted us to drive smarter. I wanted service expense to correspond better to service revenue. In short, I saw the financial benefits as the *result* of a new scheduling process, not as the objective.

I wanted us to find the buses that were not serving any purpose. The buses that puttered up and down our streets for no other reason than to employ a bus driver and because we had an extra bus in the yard. I think our folks, even the senior management people in the room, thought we would resolve our financial difficulties by asking the state to step in and bail us out, just as other public organizations had. But that was not good enough.

As the meeting progressed, I tried to drill the discussion about service delivery ever deeper. Who decides where we provide service? What goes into the decision? What causes a change? What do the customers say? What do our front-line employees, like drivers and customer service staff, say? Do we keep sending buses whether or not people get on? Do we send more buses at peak times? Fewer buses at non-peak times?

The four walls in the conference room felt like they were closing in around us. Chuck Switzer, our vice president of scheduling, started to talk about cost recovery. "Maybe if we just eliminated the buses that have a cost recovery rate below a certain level?"

Cost recovery is a transit industry term for how much money the customers pay toward the trip's actual cost. It's like the copay at a doctor's office, with public subsidies picking up the rest of the cost. Public transportation is subsidized because if we charged the trip's actual cost, very few people could afford to ride. In Rochester, the fare would have to be more than three times its current level. Thousands of people would be unable to afford the trip. They would then quit their minimum wage, entry-level jobs and go onto public assistance. In that case, the public transportation system would show a terrific cost recovery rate, but federal, state, and local government would be paying a cost exponentially higher than their subsidy of public transportation, for the public assistance of those no longer able to afford to get to work. That's why government subsidizes public transportation, at least in my opinion. Because it truly is smart government.

A company veteran, Switzer was a scheduler at heart. He made the whole system go, writing the schedules so that buses could link up at the right times and people could transfer between routes. More than Bob Frye, I felt, Chuck was trying to learn the new language I was using, but he wasn't quite getting the philosophy behind it.

Switzer and other executives in the room started working through more questions. Is our responsibility to the taxpayer? To provide bus service in the most cost-effective way possible? To do as Switzer had suggested and simply eliminate the lowest performing cost recovery routes, the routes that the taxpayers had to put the highest level of subsidy into? Or was our responsibility to our customer? To do everything we possibly could to get that entry-level employee of limited economic means to a job at a reasonable cost so that he or she wouldn't drop out and go onto public assistance, costing the taxpayer far more at the end of the day? Which should we do—deal with the routes that were producing the least amount of revenue for us, or those with the lowest ridership?

As we broke after two more hours of beating the issue from every angle imaginable, we were spent. We probably had more questions than answers. And I knew I didn't have everybody bought into the philosophy of what we were doing. Not even close.

During our next several sessions, we brought some real data to look at. We graphed. We charted. We analyzed. We graphed and charted some more. Switzer, Hendershott, Frye, and I were all in the room. I remained determined not to just cut service, and we hadn't yet come up with a solution that would somehow address our competing goals of improving both revenue and customer service, so we kept up with the work. And then the answer became clear to us. Significantly, it wasn't a senior leader who came up with it, but a mid-level employee who didn't even come from the transit world. Ryan Gallivan was a statistics guy. He had taught social studies for several years before transitioning into a role on Chuck Switzer's team in the Scheduling Department. He was still struggling to find his way in his new career, and he was about to get some big-time exposure, Pete MacNaughton style.

Meeting after meeting, Ryan and I started to click. Along with Switzer, we built from whole cloth a system that would allow us to schedule buses on the basis of both cost recovery *and* ridership levels. We took these two competing sources of information and combined them to determine when and where we'd send out our buses. Over the next several months, we designed and built what would become our nationally recognized Trip Scoring Index, or TSI.

The TSI score, given to every single bus on every single route, is comprised of two parts. The first part is the taxpayer representative side. If the bus has a zero cost recovery, then it gets a zero for that side of the equation. If it has a 100 percent cost recovery (and we have some of those), then it gets twenty-one points. The other side of the equation is the customer representative side. If the bus has nobody on board (and we have some of those), then it gets a zero. If there are forty customers on board, then it gets a 21. The TSI is calculated by marrying those numbers together. If a bus has lots of people on board and has tremendous cost recovery, its TSI is a 42. If it has

E=EFFICIENCY

CUSTOMER VOLUME SCORE		COST RECOVERY SCORE	
Customer Range	Points	Cost Recovery Range	Points
0-5	1	0-5	1
6-10	2	6-10	2
11-15	3	11-15	3
16-20	4	16-20	4
◆	◆	◆	◆
◆	◆	◆	◆
◆	◆	◆	◆
86-90	18	86-90	18
91-95	19	91-95	19
96-100	20	96-100	20

CUSTOMER VOLUME SCORE + CUSTOMER RECOVERY SCORE= TRIP SCORE

five people on board and a 15 percent cost recovery, then its TSI is a 4. TSI is the microscope that shows us where we have buses that taxpayers are disproportionately subsidizing yet are being used by very few people. These are discontinued in what amounts to a targeted, "scalpel" approach to adjusting our service.

With the advent of TSI, we had a recipe for avoiding service cuts. We wouldn't touch service that had either adequate ridership or an appreciable cost recovery. It was really unarguable. How do you argue against discontinuing service that no one or very few people are utilizing? Should you keep libraries open on Sundays if only four people are coming in to check out books? No—yet many libraries do exactly that.

Using trip scoring, we confirmed that we were indeed running routes that picked up nobody and wasted millions of taxpayer dollars a year. We were able to realize millions of dollars in savings—now more than $25 million and counting—with minimal impact on service. See the stuff you can come up with when you're not spending two years picking out bus driver uniforms? More to the point, see the kind of stuff you can come up with when you engage *all* of your employees, not merely the leadership team, around the task of delivering quality service to your customers?

THE SIMPLE ACT OF LISTENING

For me, the most gratifying consequence of listening to our employees has been seeing them so fully engaged on a daily basis around the mission of doing right by customers. Our customer service representatives work on their own to cover each other when they have to go to the bathroom, ensuring that there's enough staff on hand to answer the phones to keep on-hold times at a minimum. Our drivers now look at their quarterly report cards and realize that it truly is important that they run their routes on time. In the service building, employees recognize that getting the buses clean matters for our customers. Previously, their attitude was "Empty the fare box, make sure the oil level is high enough, and who cares whether the bus is clean or not." We existed to run buses, not think about the people who boarded them.

Most companies today focus on the customer experience. Some are good at it, but the ones that excel do so because they bring front-line and mid-level employees into the mix. We listen to what our customers tell us, but we listen with equal interest to what our employees say. Because they *both* know best. There is no better way to motivate employees to provide excellent customer service than to give them a role in designing it. Introducing a culture of no ego flowed from the corner office on down; becoming more customer centric, by contrast, needed to start with the guys scrubbing the wheel wells inside our service building and work its way up.

3.

THE BUS IS LEAVING, SO GET EVERYBODY ON BOARD!

Sell Your Organization on the New Strategic Direction

Our drivers' room is a casual and comfortable place, outfitted with tables, chairs, vending machines, and televisions. It buzzes with activity at four thirty in the morning, one in the afternoon, and again around three. At ten thirty in the morning, employees of all ages and seniority levels hang out between their runs, talking, laughing, snacking, reading the newspaper, watching television. They tend to receive me warily and reluctantly when I come to visit, and this particular day was no exception. Conversation ebbed as I waved hello and shook a few hands. I took my four quarters and put them up on the pool table. Nearby, one of our veteran drivers, the self-appointed captain of the table, was chalking up a pool cue. Sam Lopez was a Hispanic man in his mid-fifties, slender, fit, and a hard worker. "Game of eight-ball?" I asked.

He nodded and we racked the balls. He motioned for me to break, so I did, creating a mighty *crack*. Just my luck—no balls went in. It was Sam's turn. Not two minutes later, three of his striped balls were history. Bank shots. Difficult angles. This was going to go fast.

We started a casual conversation. Had he seen that Matt Damon movie, the one where he's a secret agent in Europe? Yes, but he didn't like it. Were his Yankees going to take the pennant this year? He thought so, because they had so upgraded their starting pitching. Being a die-hard Red Sox fan, I begged to differ.

I finally sunk a solid ball. Then another. Sam laughed and boasted about New York Yankees shortstop Derek Jeter. This prompted a few other drivers to come up and chime in. "Oh, the Red Sox don't stand a chance in hell," one of them said.

Sam pulled off a ridiculous shot, sinking two striped balls at once. This drew some laughter and whoops from guys around the room. Still more guys came up toward the table, probably a dozen in all. It always makes me laugh inside. These guys want to appear as if they don't care that I've come to spend time with them, but within a few minutes they all want to tell me what they think is going on. The conversation shifted to our organization—plans for salary increases, what we'd serve at our upcoming employee dinner. I nailed a few more balls, but then so did Sam. He called for the eight ball, corner pocket. Concentrating like a doctor performing open-heart surgery, he sunk that, too. Game over.

I sighed and slid more quarters onto the table. "You know," one of the drivers remarked, "we could really use some better TVs in here."

"Really," I said. "I agree, it would be great. And do you know what else would be great? If we could work together to improve our ability to announce our stops." Announcing stops was one of the measurements in our Excellence in Customer Service strategy, and the drivers were terrible at it. I regularly heard complaints at our Customer Town Meetings. The Association for the Blind and Visually Impaired brought it to our attention, as did the American Council for the Blind. Failure to announce stops was actually illegal, as it violated the Americans with Disabilities Act.

The driver who had remarked on the need for new TVs was a young, heavyset African American man named David. "See here's the thing," I said to him. "When people around here ride the bus,* you guys recognize them and make sure to announce your stops. In fact, you do it 70 percent of the time. But when we hire secret shoppers to ride the buses, they tell us that you guys are only announcing the stops 30 percent of the time."

I took balls out of the retrieval area and placed them inside the triangle so that they could be racked for a new game. By this time, all activity in the room had stopped. "Why is that?" I continued, arranging the balls in the triangle. "You guys know you're supposed to be announcing the stops. And if we're watching, you do it. But if nobody's watching, you choose not to. And someday we're going to get sued and have to spend hundreds of thousands of dollars on lawyers rather than having the money to spend on you."

David nodded his head sheepishly. "Yeah, I know." A couple of other guys affirmed their agreement.

With all the balls now back in place in the triangle, I positioned them on the table, removed the triangle, and nodded to Sam to break. "I'll make you a deal," I said to David and the guys standing around him. "You get your announcement of stops to hit 50 percent in the next quarter, and we'll put two really big, nice flat-screen TVs in the drivers' room."

"Really? Two?" David asked.

Sam broke the balls with a loud crack.

"Absolutely," I said.

"Surround sound?" one of the drivers asked.

I smiled. "Don't push your luck."

When trying to turn around a company and achieve sustainable success, managers can't work too hard to keep an organization focused on strategy. We can't just have employees mechanically enact strategy; we need them to contribute proactively. So many turnarounds fail because senior managers don't work hard enough to get employees invested. Leaders give big speeches, they promulgate

---

*All of our employees, myself included, are required to ride the bus once a month.

strategy in employee newsletters, and they offer reminders of strategy by having posters put up on the walls. While all that is important, we've got to take advantage of every opportunity, big and small, to teach people about the strategy, to show them how it translates into their daily lives, and to get them bought in and excited.

Our drivers wound up not getting the televisions. But today, they do understand that they need to keep their buses on time to help us realize Excellence in Customer Service. Our accounts receivable employees understand how important it is that our subsidy partners meet their financial commitments to achieve our strategic goal of Long-Term Financial Success. Our human resources team recognizes the importance of an integrated annual review process to enable employees to work to their full potential (our strategy of Employee Success). We've become an organization working full throttle to achieve a purpose. Against the odds, we've become a destination-driven organization with a workforce fully invested in driving to that destination. And that has helped us become what everyone wants to be—a high-performance organization.

A SUNDAY AFTERNOON DRIVE

When I was growing up, every once in a while we'd feel pretty caught up on farm work, and as a reward my parents would pile all four of us kids into the backseat of our 1969 Chevy Malibu and take us for a Sunday drive. Mom would sit in the passenger seat, and Dad would drive us through backcountry roads in upstate New York. Dust would billow as pavement turned to crumbled rock and rutted dirt roads. It was pleasant—a listless, purposeless meandering. Sometimes we'd stop for ice cream or to skip rocks in a stream. We just went wherever Dad decided to drive us, taking whichever random turns he saw fit to make.

This is exactly what used to happen at the RGRTA. Every day for years, we functioned as a company going on a Sunday afternoon drive—listless, purposeless, with a leadership arbitrarily making decisions on the basis of executive whim. What made for a nice Sunday afternoon as a kid worked less well for an entire organization. It was easy for my dad to keep everyone on board, because we all sat in the backseat. Not so easy when you have 750 employees spread over nine campuses working three shifts.*

A few examples should help evoke the serious drawbacks inherent in the "Sunday Drive" approach to business As of this writing, we're getting ready to expand our main campus in the city of Rochester. Unlike so many organizations, we've expanded the business in recent years, and we need more room for new buses and employees. We're beginning the process of acquiring multiple parcels on the western part of our campus that is currently occupied by several old, triple-decker residential houses. We're eyeing that land as a potential parking area for employees. We've identified funding for the project, we know how we're going to use the properties, and we've got a schedule for acquiring, demolishing, and rebuilding that best advances our need for parking. All before we even hired a Realtor.

Compare this to ten years ago. At that time, a property owner on the other side of our campus approached us to see if we wanted to buy an adjacent property. A good ten structures stood there, mainly decrepit drug houses. The Authority bought the house of the guy who had knocked on our door. Then we bought another one. And another. Ultimately, we acquired all the properties on one side of our campus and demolished them, spending more than a half million dollars. Yet we got no benefit from that. For ten years, all we did was cut the grass. The property had been purchased with no funding in place, no plan, and no schedule to make improvements. It's an example of purposeless decision-making with no destination in mind, and our organization was rife with it.

---

*In 2004. We now have 820 employees.

In the old days, the Authority installed bus shelters at specific locations because an elected official or somebody else requested it— not because we had a system to ensure that the most active bus stops had shelters. In fact, if you called up and asked us for a bus shelter back then, chances are good you would have gotten one, to the tune of $15,000. A senior executive would just call up the operations staff and say, "Put a bus shelter here, put a bus shelter there." The result was chaos and poor service for our customers. We discovered instances of stops with shiny new bus shelters where only two or three customers waited, whereas at other stops eighty or ninety customers stood out in the bitter cold, simply because nobody had called. There was no map in place to guide employees. We were just driving.

The haphazard "Sunday Drive" approach had some other unfortunate ramifications. Beyond the worker demoralization and fear that came with paternalism generally, the lack of a perceptible strategy meant that our people couldn't connect their work with any longer-term ambition or objective. They didn't see their work's relevance or purpose. In addition, our organization was forced to manage reactively.

In the bus shelter example, for instance, the decision to locate a bus shelter was made in reaction to a customer request, or even worse, just plain old politics; organizational insight and wisdom never moved beyond our day-to-day delivery of service.

Consider how we decided to buy our first state-of-the-art bus simulator. In 2001, we picked up intelligence that a local TV station was planning a story exposing our drivers for speeding and running red lights. So we arranged a news conference to get out in front of that story. Before microphones and flashing bulbs, the company announced the purchase of a $250,000 bus simulator as evidence of the effort we put into training our operators. We did buy that simulator, the sole purpose of which was to inoculate ourselves against bad PR. Now, it's not that it was a bad idea to buy a simulator; that device could well fit into a very sound strategy of saving money by avoiding accidents caused by poorly trained drivers, or as part of a strategy to serve customers better. But in the world of yesteryear, this money was spent in reaction to a potential news story (which by the way never aired!).

Ultimately, the "Sunday Drive" approach fails an organization because it provides no mechanism or logic for distinguishing between good ideas an executive might have and bad ones. As a youngster, I found driving without purpose fun, but the downside was that sometimes my dad would take a wrong turn and run into a dead end. Then we'd have to drive all the way back, hoping we didn't run out of gas or get lost before the sun went down. The same thing happens in an organizational context—which is why we wound up with a $27.7 million projected shortfall.

> **The "Sunday Drive" approach fails an organization because it provides no mechanism or logic for distinguishing between good ideas an executive might have and bad ones.**

Let's suppose 80 percent of a leader's ideas are good, and 20 percent are bad. These days, we have a strategic development and execution process in place to filter out most if not all of those 20 percent. During the "Sunday Drive" days, no such sieve existed—no process obligated us to ask why we would take an action we were considering—and 100 percent of the ideas got implemented. Our decision to purchase drug houses might have had some logic behind it, but it left us at a dead end and damn near out of gas in the dark.

Or take our 1957 bus. Back around 2002, the company got a letter from someone who had been driving through the hills of Pennsylvania and spotted a decrepit 1957 GMC model, the same kind driven in Rochester's streets a generation earlier. Pretty neat, right? Without much thought, we dispatched several maintenance staff to inspect the bus, purchase it for several thousand dollars, and have it flatbedded back to Rochester. We then pondered how to use the bus and began a multi-year effort to retrofit and restore it, spending more than $150K. When I became CEO, I immediately discontinued this project-without-a-purpose.

WHY DO WE HAVE COWS ANYWAY?

When I was a kid, we would get up in the morning, rub the sleep from our eyes, brush our teeth, pull on barn clothes, and go out and do two hours of chores, to feed the cows and other animals. I resented like hell that the cows ate and the shit got shoveled before I got to eat or take a shower. But that was why we were there. For the cows.

I expect my parents didn't design it that way to send a message, but they certainly could have. Why were we there? To take care of the cows. Simple plan. Everything falls in place from there.

We didn't go on vacation. Because we had to take care of the cows.

We didn't get new bikes. We needed money for grain for the cows.

We had to be home from school by four o'clock. So we could put the cows in the barn.

During the summer of 2005, I gathered a half dozen of our senior managers together at a local college with a private sector change consultant. Our mission: to develop a vision and strategic focus. We had introduced our Driving Excellence initiative in 2004, but that had only been a tactic. By the summer of 2005, I had realized that before we could even tackle the problem of getting our whole organization aligned and working toward a common purpose, we needed to develop our mission, vision, and strategies— essentially, reinvent ourselves along the model of a private company. And in the midst of our financial crisis, we needed to do it fast. We'd have to put ourselves through a business-redesign boot camp during which we'd take our company apart and build it back together again in a more meaningful and sustainable way. Over the course of a couple of days, we'd have to define our organizational purpose, answering, as I like to call it, the cow question: Why do we have cows anyway?

I scheduled two full-day sessions one after the other. I intended to ask our team a basic question: What do we do? You can ask it of any organization. Private, public, not-for-profit. What do we do?

If you gather a cross-section of your employees from all across the organizational chart, typically one of your department heads will speak first because they're accustomed to being around the boss. "We educate young people," they'll say. Or: "We provide public safety and patrol the streets." Or maybe: "We pick up people on our buses and take them places."

Then your workers will start to speak, once they've come to see they're not in your office to get fired. They'll start to throw out a bunch of programs to you. "We run the Jobs First program to help people find work." "We try to improve the standardized test scores for our students." "We make widgets to sell to people."

See the disconnect? Your department heads are listing the purpose for which your company, agency, or nonprofit is responsible, while your workers think that they work to keep the programs going.

We gathered in a large conference room overlooking a sprawling college campus about thirty miles outside of Rochester. Bob Frye was one of the leadership team executives who joined us. After several months trying to figure out what to do with Frye, I had finally decided the summer before to keep him on. But with conditions. First and foremost, Bob had to stick close to his role as CFO and restrain himself from meddling in areas unrelated to financial operations. As I put it, he had to "swim in his own lane." Also, I reduced his salary. I reorganized his staff so that fewer employees reported to him. I moved his office. With these measures, I hoped to send strong messages to him and his colleagues. Bob Frye was not going to be the same old Bob Frye anymore. I really wondered if he'd even stay.

Our facilitator led us through an exercise where we pretended that we were on the hit television show *The Apprentice*. Donald Trump had decided that there was money to be made in a transportation system in our community. For purposes of the exercise, we skipped the market research phase, assuming that Trump had already done his homework and determined that there was a market for our product. The question was this: If Donald Trump gave us seed money, how would we go about building a company in our market to achieve his vision? How would we set it up? What would our mission and vision be?

We wanted to let our imaginations run wild, and so we tried to forget about all the real-life issues that made up the day-to-day experience of running our existing company—the departments, the programs we ran, the union regulations, the bureaucracy that existed, the regulatory agencies we had to please, the political pressures we faced. Some folks at the table had trouble with this; they started to talk about a particular regulation, or how we got money this way or that. Steve Hendershott started to give us history lessons on why we had been forced to decide in the past to take certain actions. We rejected that kind of discussion. This is Donald Trump's company. Do you think he wants to hear that some government regulation prevents us from closing down a garage in a certain section of the city? Do you think Trump wants to get a report that says we can't fix the buses at night because our unionized mechanics have always fixed them during the day?

Another person at the table that day was our vice president of human resources, Debbie Griffith. Debbie is the first and only person I have ever hired on the spot. When I met and interviewed her, I knew she was perfect for our team. Thin, stylishly dressed, with shortish blond hair, Debbie was always trying to move the conversation to a higher level. It took a while for her to feel comfortable leaving county government, where she had worked for more than twenty years, but ultimately she decided to take on the challenge of transforming an organization.

It was Debbie who said, "We pick up people on buses and take them places. That's what we do. Period."

Indeed. That *was* what we did. That, in its most basic form, was our mission.

As the morning ran on, our Donald Trump team worked to narrow down the list of concrete things we required to deliver on that mission. We realized that to bring our product to market, we needed, in essence, four things: (1) a bus, (2) someone to drive the bus, (3) some system to tell the bus driver where to go, and (4) some system to tell people where the bus was going and when, so they could get on it. That's it. It wasn't about procurement, or insurance, or human resources, or operations. All that stuff was bureaucracy that had been built up over the years.

It was a fascinating process. We were asking ourselves the most basic of questions: Why do we have cows? What should we feed them? How often? We were stripping away our operation so that we could then figure out what we really needed to do to make what we did even better—and sustainable.

Okay, so we needed a bus. Should we buy it or lease it? Should we buy it new or used? How long should we keep it? I didn't know the answer to these questions any more than other people at the table did.

We needed a bus driver. Should he or she be our employee? Or should we outsource the employees? Should we train them? Or should we let them come to us already trained by outsourcing that function?

We needed a schedule. Some way to determine where the bus was going to go. How should we decide? If Donald Trump was going to start selling a product, what would he do? He'd check to see if someone wanted to buy it, right? Exactly.

And we needed to tell people how to get on board our bus. Printed schedules? A website? TV and radio advertising? Ads on the sides of the buses? All of the above?

We sell bus rides. Who wants to buy them? Where do they want to get on the bus? Where do they want to go? How long are they willing to let the trip take? What will the marketplace allow us to price it at?

In finding our core mission and how to perform it, we became ever more aware that the inefficient bureaucracy that had grown up over the years needed to be cut back. Let me speak to this problem for a moment, since I anticipate it to be an important one for many troubled organizations.

Tom Daschle, the United States senator from South Dakota who went on to become majority leader, once remarked that we as Americans needed to protect the public education system. He said this during a speech in which he opposed President George W. Bush's proposal to allow parents to use school vouchers. Say that again, Senator Daschle? We need to protect the public education system? Since when do we have to protect the system? I thought the purpose of schools was to educate kids. To prepare them for adulthood. Or for a job. I'm not sure when the purpose of schools became to protect the public education system. Talk about a dog chasing its tail.

As we discussed what could be changed in our own organization, Frye was the first to raise his hand; he stated that employee salaries were the most expensive. Hendershott said he thought fuel was a huge expense, and perhaps we could better manage that. Then Debbie said that health care costs were out of control and perhaps we could negotiate with our union to reduce those expenses. Our director of vehicle maintenance, Jerry Siconolfi, made an impassioned plea that buying bus parts was really expensive, especially since they are a petroleum-based product and the price of a barrel of oil was through the roof.

"Look," Frye said. "This is not difficult. Payroll is our biggest expense by far. We're a service organization. Seventy-five percent of our expense is in people. We're going to have to reduce employees."

Siconolfi had on a short-sleeve shirt showing off his beefy forearms. He responded by going right back to the mechanics. "I don't disagree with what Bob says, but maybe we concentrate that in the maintenance area by working to reduce overtime."

I was growing frustrated. Before our break, we had been thinking at the forty-thousand-foot level, but now we were back talking about ground-level tactics. At this rate, we'd never come up with a clear and inspiring path to change. We had answered why we had cows, but we hadn't answered what the most expensive part of taking care of them was, and this was critical to understanding why we were almost out of hay. It also seemed like so many of the people that I had gathered were striving to prove their knowledge, leadership, and understanding of their respective responsibilities. I'm not quite certain that anyone, perhaps with the exception of Frye, had a real appreciation of the scope of the pending crisis, even though they'd seen the numbers many times. Public agencies that provide a public service always gets bailed out, right? So we had some problems. Big deal. Someone would save us. They always had in the past.

I had scheduled two sessions of strategy development because I was hoping some of the thinking we generated the first day would germinate overnight and yield new insights. Early the second morning, I got up and went for a run. It was deep summer in New York State's Finger Lakes region, and I've always loved how the sun comes up early, and in the humid air you can just smell all that the day has in store. As I started along the shores of Conesus Lake, I ran past a gravel road up a hill, the flat, calm lake to my left. You could hear the distant buzz of fishing boats. The scent of extinguished camp-fires lingered in the air. As I turned and jogged along a road hugging the lakeshore, passing small white summer cottages, it came to me. Everyone had been right that wages, health care, fuel, and bus parts were our greatest expenses. But there was something more fundamental at work here. And as I now saw, it had to do with something we talked about in the last chapter: the way we scheduled our buses. I quickened my pace as I looped back toward my house. I couldn't wait to get back in for our second day.

Debbie Griffith and Jerry Siconolfi were already in the conference room at the college when I got there. As the others arrived, I could sense how much they were not looking forward to a second day of this. I sat down, making a point of not occupying the head of the table. I readjusted my seat, smoothed the front of my golf shirt, and plunged right in. "In our business," I said, "we drive buses and pick people up, right?"

I looked around the table for reaction. They nodded in agreement.

"And four times a year, our people sit down and determine where the buses are going to go and how often they'll go there. In other words, they lay out the schedule."

Again they nodded.

"And the schedule determines how many drivers we need, and how much we'll have to pay them. Bob, that was your conclusion, as I recall." I looked at him, prompting him to nod. "The schedule determines how many miles that we'll drive and how many hours the bus will need to be running. The direct result being how much fuel we will need. Steve, that was what you thought." I made eye contact with him, and then I turned to our vice president of human resources. "And Debbie, the number of bus drivers will absolutely determine how much our health care expenses will be. And the number of buses that we need will directly result in how much our repair bill will be and how much we'll spend on parts, as Jerry Siconolfi knows all too well." Jerry's face lit up in a broad smile with my recognizing the challenges he faced every day. "Yet there's a more basic question: What determines the schedule?"

"That's easy," Frye said. "How many people want to go to which places."

"Precisely. And that gets us to our real answer. Given what we've been doing with Trip Scoring, we need to put our buses where people want to go, when they want to go there."

Debbie shot me a skeptical look. "Well, why did we bother to work on Trip Scoring to begin with?"

I nodded at her. "That's exactly the point. I screwed up. We did Trip Scoring without having an underlying strategy in place. And this is that strategy." Inside, I also realized that I had put my finger on a big reason for my conflict with Bob Frye. His strategy was to save money and mine was to drive efficiency. What we lacked was a common strategic goal that would unify these: Putting Buses Where People Want to Go, When They Want to Go There. It became one of the three pillars in our initial Strategic Plan.

The customers decided how many buses we would have. And the number of buses would determine how many drivers we needed. Not the schedule. For decades, the schedule had determined the number of buses and drivers we had. We had been doing it Tom Daschle style, protecting the system rather than achieving the purpose. If we had gotten rid of half the cows on the farm, we wouldn't have kept putting in five thousand bales of hay. That would have been wasting gas, seed, and insurance. We put in enough hay to feed the size herd we had. The herd drove the process, not the hay.

Working through our analysis in regards to Putting Buses Where People Want to Go, When They Want to Go There helped meet a major short-term objective: solving a massive operating shortfall. That objective in turn became enshrined in our Strategic Plan's next pillar—Achieve Financial Stability (in subsequent years, for reasons we'll explore later, we would come to call this "Long-Term Financial Success"). It would be great if we could more efficiently use our buses and work to reduce the visual stigma associated with under-utilized transit vehicles, and we knew that there would be sizeable financial benefit from doing exactly that. But we still weren't done defining our strategy. We knew that we also needed a longer-term plan to significantly alter our position in the community. We wanted it to be something we could be passionate about. Something that would make us an industry leader in our commitment and focus. Something to motivate our employees, engage the community, and excite our customers.

We went back to the basics once again. We needed those same four things to perform our mission: a bus, someone to drive the bus, some system to tell the bus driver where to go, and some system to tell people where the bus was going and when, so they could get on it. We were missing the fourth piece of the puzzle: a system that would tell both customers and potential customers where the bus was going. Simple as can be. And that led to the third pillar in our now days-old Strategic Plan: Excellence in Customer Service.

There we had it. Our Strategic Plan in three simple statements. Putting Buses Where People Want to Go, When They Want to Go There. Achieve Financial Stability. And Excellence in Customer Service. In 2007, we'd add a fourth pillar—Employee Participation. Initially, though, our plan came from the most basic elements of what we needed to bring our product to the marketplace. And it was easily understood by everyone. Now there was just one little thing left to do. We had to execute it. And we had to succeed. Winter was closing in fast.

GETTING EVERYBODY ON BOARD

I remember those rare occasions when my dad would get up at the crack of dawn and announce that we were going to the Great Escape theme park on Lake George that day. The passion with which my younger brother Charlie and I then did our farm chores was unbelievable. We fed the cows faster, cleaned the barn better, and threw down the hay from the mow to the barn floor with much greater purpose. If someone announced the destination (and even further, if the destination represented a clear personal reward for labor that we put in), our car ride had some purpose. We knew we were going to enjoy the fruits of our labor.

So that's what we did first at the Authority: We announced the destination, starting with our board. They needed to know the size and scope of the financial problem. They had been told before I got there, but they hadn't focused on the issue, and since their CEO at the time hadn't made a big deal out of it, or laid out an aggressive course of action, they essentially ignored it.

With an issue this significant, putting it in front of any group of people once is not going to get it done. You need to come back, time and again, to make people focus on the issue's importance. If we were going to turn on the engines and start taking the organization in a particular direction, let alone a new direction, they needed to know why such dramatic action was necessary. In September 2005, after several sessions of putting our short- and long-term financial position in front of the board, we gathered them in an off-site session about forty-five minutes outside of downtown Rochester.

The senior management group laid out for the board the full financial picture for the current fiscal year, and projections for the next three years. Then we laid out our Strategic Plan. Our *first* Strategic Plan. And we described the very specific steps we would be taking immediately to address our financial calamity and implement our bold customer service vision.

The dialogue between the board and our management group was outstanding. They challenged our assumptions, questioned our initiatives, and applauded our planning process and strategic thinking. "This is fantastic stuff," our new chairman, John Doyle, said. "You've clearly given us a lot to chew on, and we can tell there's now a direction in which to drive." All during the meeting, I kept eyeing Bob Frye, who was seated at a forty-five-degree angle to my right, strangely silent. I couldn't tell what he was thinking.

We broke that night around eight o'clock, and I was one of the last people to leave. "Hey, Mark, hold on," someone said in the restaurant lobby. It was Bob. He walked over and gave me a hug, tears in his eyes. He was clearly struck by the significance, depth, and focus of our day with the board. "I am so proud of you," he said. "I am so proud of what we are doing. I can't believe how far we've come in such a short time. Whether we get through this or not, we've given ourselves a fighting chance. I am just loving the opportunity to be a part of this."

I was stunned. I had sensed that he was growing more open to change. But nothing like this. It was so gratifying to realize that he was fully on board.

Even with him and the board aligned behind the strategy, we had another, even harder task: announcing the strategy to our employees. The union leadership's general attitude toward life on the job back in those days went roughly as follows: We come in to work. And you're going to pay us. And however much you pay us, we're going to complain about it. And don't even think about measuring our performance. We want 100 percent of our health care paid for, but that doesn't count as a benefit. We want to be able to not show up for eighteen days in a year, without being sick or on vacation—just not show up—before you can discipline us. We want to be able to take days off, even if we don't have any vacation days. Sick days will be like vacation days. And we'll deliver the product in twice the amount of time at four times the cost of the private sector. And don't tell us anything about tough times. There's always been plenty of money. There will always be plenty of money. Just pay us more. Pay us at the highest level of the industry, for mediocre work.

In short, this was a pretty tough workforce to turn around and get aligned behind a strategy. My approach again was to repeat and reinforce our strategic pillars. We did the posters on the wall and the employee newsletters. Yet we also supplemented those with a company blog and with distribution of an annual Comprehensive Plan that clearly laid out our pillars and assessed our performance against those pillars. We also stressed our strategic pillars at every employee meeting and at mid-level meetings across our organization. Again and again. Day in and day out.

Pounding in the strategy doesn't have to be tedious or tense. When companies send us tickets to go to a baseball game or the zoo, we have a trivia contest where my assistant April will put up, via email, questions related to our annual Comprehensive Plan and employees have to answer questions about our strategies and last quarter results. The first employee to answer the questions correctly wins the tickets. It's not a giveaway; there are no free turkeys or plates of ribs. You have to know about our strategy to get the tickets.

Walk around our facilities, and you'll also see our performance scorecards up everywhere, relaying actual results against the four strategic pillars. What we've done is give each of our strategies a color. Yellow stands for Achieve Financial Stability (now called Long-Term Financial Success); green, Excellence in Customer Service; blue, Employee Participation (now called Employee Success); and red, Connecting to Communities (a newer version of Putting Buses Where People Want to Go, When They Want to Go There). The data aside, people are reminded of our strategies in a cognitively powerful way every fifteen seconds when walking around. Everyone—bus operators, radio controllers, customer service personnel, up to and including the vice presidents—is nudged to tie our strategies to the most basic task they happen to be performing minute to minute.

Some of the practices we've discussed in the first two chapters also help us reinforce our strategies in employees' minds. Year in and year out, employees are already primed to accept our strategies because of all the time we spend soliciting their feedback about market conditions. As mentioned in Chapter One, we also engage employees in our ongoing refinement of the strategies themselves. Finally, we construct and lay out our Comprehensive Plan in a way that encourages employees to read it. Because the plan includes so many pictures of our employees, and because we also talk throughout the plan about their role in developing and advancing strategy, people go to the book looking for their and their friends' pictures, even referring jokingly to the book as the "high school yearbook." It's a small thing, but if it gets people to think seriously about strategy, then it's a big help.

TALKING THE WALK

Getting people to think strategically requires not merely getting them to agree on a conscious level to whatever path your organization is on, but training them to change the very way they conceive of and speak about their daily work. As managers, we're used to crafting what we say, but we don't always ensure that carefully crafted language trickles down into the culture of our organizations. That's a mistake. To fight off impending financial ruin, we also mobilized an extremely powerful, simple, yet grossly underutilized tool: words.

Ronald Reagan recognized the special power of words to reframe reality when he made a special effort to use positive language in speeches designed to be inspiring or uplifting—speaking about "remembering something" rather than "never forgetting." Think of what it means when you tell your grandmother that you'll always remember those special Sunday dinners at her home (as opposed to never forgetting them). Bill Clinton understood this power, too, when he talked about getting people to "invest" rather than "spend."

As I've seen firsthand in politics, words can sometimes mean the difference between winning and losing. When I worked for a member of Congress, I saw how useful it was for the right to refer to the leadership of organized labor as "union bosses" as opposed to "union leaders" or "union thugs." At the same time, the left wing positioned itself to win in the gun control debate during the early 1990s by talking about banning "assault weapons" as opposed to "firearms" or "automatic weap-

Words can sometimes mean the difference between winning and losing.

ons." Who would come out in opposition to banning "assault"? Once the label was in place, the debate was over.

When I became CEO, the vocabulary at our company was scattered and pretty meaningless—as unorganized as a Sunday afternoon drive. Now that we were adopting private-sector thinking, however, we needed to instill some linguistic order, and for that we turned to the business world, too.

Beyond speaking of *customers*, as private companies do, our Excellence in Customer Service pillar prompted us to provide a *product* instead of what we had always provided—a "service." Our staff didn't use the word "service" in the same way that many people in the business community use it today. Rather, they used it, perhaps surprisingly, as a way to not even think about serving actual paying customers— "service" in the sense of a Soviet-style provision of the State. It's the same as the town clerk's office that stays open only from nine to four—that's the "service" they offer. But in reality they're only serving themselves. It's *convenient* for them to be open from nine to four, but not for most customers, who have to work during that time period.

Since 2004, we've also adopted *cash registers* to replace the conventional "fare box." "Fare box" conveys a public sector mind-set, whereas *cash register* helps our people understand that the people riding the bus are putting money into a cash register just as they do at any private business—in other words, they are paying customers with a choice. Traditionally, many of our drivers who thought in terms of "fare box" would allow friends and family to board the bus without paying. By helping our drivers understand that they had a *cash register* in front of them, we were cementing the notion that they were providing a quality experience worth paying for—and an experience they couldn't just give away for free, either.

Excellence in Customer Service, then, wasn't just a strategy—it entailed a whole new way of thinking. We didn't drive "buses" around the city any longer; we drove *stores*. And once you start to think of a "bus" as a *store* offering an experience, all sorts of things become possible. Cleaner stores, so that customers feel more comfortable. Stores whose doors open on time, so that customers can rely on that store to fill their needs.

The name of our second strategic pillar, "Putting Buses Where People Want to Go, When They Want to Go There," might seem like a rather straightforward, even elementary phrasing. That was intentional. If we had embraced business-speak and called this the "Productivity" pillar or the "Private Sector Mind-set" strategy, many in our workforce might not have understood what that meant. If we had called it "Rewriting the Schedules," people wouldn't have understood the greater significance of what we were trying to pull off. The language of "Putting Buses Where People Want to Go, When They Want to Go There" got the message right, in a format everyone could understand. It proved so powerful that it helped us win over even our most hardened, militant drivers. They couldn't disagree that this strategic pillar was a smart idea. Who could defend driving huge buses around our community where people didn't want to go, when they didn't want to go there?

Advancing "Putting Buses Where People Want to Go, When They Want to Go There" meant introducing a number of new, supportive words and phrases into our corporate lexicon, chief among them *productivity*. The public sector hardly talks about productivity. By contrast, our company talks about productivity all the time, whether in relation to our measurement systems or to the product profile we offer. Speaking of productivity has gotten our employees away from thinking that they need to act as protectors of existing service.

Talking about productivity leads us naturally to discuss Trip Scoring, the analytical tool we use to drive productivity. Ryan Gallivan, formerly one of our mid-level scheduling guys, explains: "We built the word 'trip' into the term because it was important to get the analysis down to the level of individual trips, assessing how each bus was performing." Today, we rarely look to modify an entire route, but rather trips that are not adequately serving the community's needs, or trips that are too crowded. "Scoring" is critical because we wanted to demonstrate that the score of each bus will be the measurement device to determine whether to add or subtract service.

What results from Trip Scoring and a focus on productivity? One thing's for sure: It ain't "service cuts." Rather, it's *adjustments* in our product. In 2009, as public subsidy revenues declined and expenses rose, I watched brutal public hearings in which leaders of public agencies defended their proposed "service cuts." In fact, 84 percent of transit systems in the country were poised to enact either drastic fare increases or service cuts.* All these leaders were doing was making wholesale, across-the-board cuts in service. But cuts don't help anyone. By comparison, we have a process that commits us to driving efficiency and productivity, and that allows us to balance our responsibilities to both customers and taxpayers.

I can't tell you how many times I've spoken about our business philosophy at national events and had the graybeards say, "Oh, that's just a fancy way of cutting service." Well, we're not the ones who have these ugly hearings. We'd argue we haven't cut service once, just made it more efficient. I've seen transit systems that will eliminate service where they were driving fifty miles and only picking up one person. And they call that cutting service. We think it's foolish to call it that. To be running a bus fifty miles for one person is stupid in the first place.

"Cuts" implies that all you are doing is taking something away from customers. *Adjustments* can mean adding routes, too, which is what we frequently do. When our senior leadership meets on a quarterly basis to evaluate our service profile, we discuss underperforming trips but also routes where we don't have enough service on the street, and we then analyze how we can alter schedule times to improve performance. Speaking of *adjustments* gets us away from

---

*"APTA: 84 Percent of Transit Systems Raising Fares, Cutting Service," April 1, 2010.

the mind-set of making wholesale changes to our routes—namely cuts—without being mindful of what the community's actual needs are. In instances when we need to pare back a bus trip, we'll even ride the buses with our customers and query them as to which alternative route schedule they'd prefer. Because we're not wasting money driving around empty buses, we have the resources to better serve routes where fifty people are waiting to get on a bus.

The traditional transit funding model.

Our financial focus joined with our emphasis on customer service brought yet another important term into our lexicon, *taxpayer reliance* instead of the standard "cost recovery." The dollar you put into our cash register contributes to what we call "cost recovery." People in our industry use "cost recovery" to designate that percentage of expenses covered by the fare-paying public. The difference between full expense and cost recovery is taxpayer subsidies. We prefer to talk about *taxpayer reliance* because if you're focused on "cost recovery," your first reaction as an organization is always to raise fares on customers. By focusing on reducing our reliance on taxpayer subsidies, we can orient ourselves toward searching for alternative revenue sources instead of just jacking fares. This might seem like a trivial change in language, yet the underlying difference in thinking has probably done more than anything else to put us in a place where we can cut our fares at times when the overwhelming majority of transit systems are raising theirs. Because we focus on reducing reliance on taxpayer subsidies, we go out and find business partners—or as we call them, *subsidy*

$$\frac{Farebox}{Revenue} + \frac{Subsidy}{Partners} + \frac{Taxpayer}{Subsidies} = \frac{FULL}{COST}$$

Our new business model to reduce reliance on taxpayer dollars.

partners—throughout the community to help fund our service rather than go to our core customers with our hand out.

As mentioned, in 2007 we added a fourth pillar, what we initially called "Employee Participation." We felt that it was important to build one of our key strategies directly around our employees. Even before we adopted this pillar, though, we embraced a number of words designed to encourage engagement in the workplace. For instance, we began identifying members of our workforce as *team members* rather than the standard "staff members." When I was a twenty-five-year-old kid working as assistant to the town supervisor in the suburban town of Chili, New York, all the local town supervisors met at a town hall to discuss a major sales tax litigation issue. My boss couldn't go, so I represented him there. One of the local newspapers came and took a picture of all of us meeting. The caption identified all these town supervisors by name and me as a "Chili staffer." A local political figure pointed this phrasing out to me several weeks later, smugly noting that I was only a "staffer." It stuck with me how derisive he intended that description to feel.

Our transition to *team members* got people to realize that they should work on the same level, as colleagues, regardless of where they sit in the organizational structure. And as we saw in Chapter One, I'm literally talking about sitting. Senior leaders shouldn't feel they deserve to have $700 chairs while their colleague is sitting in a $50 chair. At the same time, the guy or gal sitting in a $50 chair is more inclined to focus on organizational success if the whole issue of status isn't present as a distraction. A "staff member" is working to allow his or her boss to have fame and glory; a *team member* is working to create an environment in which everybody gets to rush the pitcher's mound and drink champagne.

> **A *team member* is working to create an environment in which everybody gets to rush the pitcher's mound and drink champagne.**

While many companies pay out "bonuses," "extra pay," or "extra compensation," we offer *incentive compensation*, because the object is to urge our employees to realize our strategic obligations. "Bonuses" can be arbitrary, whereas *incentives* are tied to very specific performance measures. We prefer *incentive compensation* over "performance incentives," to highlight the idea that employees are being compensated for the effort they put in—again, a direct linkage between organizational and personal success.

We also have come to speak of ourselves as possessing *administrative* employees rather than "non-union" employees. Formerly, the union/non-union distinction reigned supreme, and as a result an employee's status as part of collective bargaining or outside it comprised a key part of his or her identity. We wanted to downplay that point of demarcation because we were trying to get people to put the organization first in their minds instead of some other loyalty, such as loyalty to a union. Better to refer to our white collar workforce by their function—*administrative* employees. Relatedly, we talk about *our employees* instead of "union members." Remember Frank Falzone? He was the thick-necked, mustached, heavyset business agent for the union. He kept confronting and interrupting me at our employee meetings as a means of playing to the union members. He'd always talk about "our members." I'd correct him by saying, "You mean our employees." Using this language constantly reminded the members of the workforce watching our exchange that they were first and foremost *our employees*, not his "members."

Beyond instilling language around our strategic pillars, we've taken care to evolve the words we use to name and define the pillars themselves. The first moniker we came up with for our financial pillar was "Achieve Financial Stability." We chose "achieve" because the scary squiggly things under the rocks clearly demonstrated our deficiencies; our report card was of the sort that you'd be afraid to bring home to Mom, and we wanted one good enough to post on the fridge. We chose "financial" to focus everyone on the importance of money, and "stability" because we wanted to enjoy enough protection so that our financial need wouldn't force us into making abrupt, immediate decisions. Achieving financial stability would give us the flexibility we needed to pursue longer-term strategies.

Within two years, our new business approach had begun to show results, so we changed the name of our financial pillar to "Maintain Financial Stability." This was a big deal for us; despite the odds, we'd gotten straight A's on our report card the last eight quarters, and now it was time to acknowledge that milestone. By Year Five of our transition, we changed our pillar once again to "Long-Term Financial Success." We wanted to convey our new determination to make decisions that were in our best long-term interests. We also wanted to focus on being successful—meeting our financial obligations, preserving funds to guard against potential future instability, covering our employees health care expenses, meeting our pension obligations, not incurring debt—rather than remaining "stable."

I can summarize what's happened in our company around language by observing that in our culture just as in our operations, we're no longer a traditional public agency. We're a public-private hybrid. We don't think of ourselves as an agency, and we don't talk about ourselves that way, either. We think and talk of "running our business."

Of course, language itself is not enough. There must be dozens of transit companies in the world that refer to their passengers as customers. But many of these companies haven't worked to incorporate infrastructure or cultural change to get people to see riders as customers. All they've done is play superficially with words. I call it bumper-sticker talk. Cutesy, catchy little phrases that make for a good sound bite, but with no ass-in-your-pants structural change to support it. Yet words are not foundational—the infrastructure supporting change is. Just putting Wheaties in a differently designed box doesn't get you anything (although, of course, changing the cereal without changing the box won't take you so far, either). When you change the two together—now you're making progress.

Cutesy, catchy little phrases that make for a good sound bite, but with no ass-in-your-pants structural change to support it.

Instilling a strategic focus through attention to language is a gradual and sometimes painful process. I remember one leadership team meeting in the summer of 2005 when Chuck Switzer, our twenty-five-year veteran vice president of scheduling, was leading a discussion on the results of our new Trip Scoring Index. As he stood up to talk, you could see him struggling to select the right words as he was articulating his department's new thought process of scheduling buses in a customer-centric fashion. "So, um, well, we're looking to make, um, *adjustments* to the serv—I mean product—we're going to put out for this coming, uh, what do we call it?"

"A quarter, Chuck," I said, laughing.

"Right, the coming quarter."

Everybody else started to laugh.

"Hey, I'm trying," Chuck said, cracking a grin himself.

And that's all you can ask. People trying hard to learn, a little bit each day. When a grizzled old veteran like Chuck, with an abacus back in his desk drawer, was working hard to match his language with his actions, you knew there was hope.

THE BEST BARN CHORES EVER

Understanding the broader strategy helps people accept change— even when change is scary. It's much easier to accept something new and unfamiliar when you can perceive an underlying logic at work. Our plan to redo route scheduling so that our buses took people where they wanted to go, when they wanted to go there was not too popular with the drivers. Tensions crested three weeks before Labor Day 2005. Chuck Switzer's Scheduling Department normally took all the different routes and used scheduling software to break them into individual pieces, taking into account the union work rules. Then the drivers would gather in the drivers' room—the same place where Sam Lopez kicked my ass in pool—and select which work they wanted to perform for the coming quarter. Remember, the schedule drove the system. Not customers. It had worked this way for years. Tom Daschle would have loved it.

At this particular meeting, hundreds of bus drivers gathered in the drivers' room to go through this process, and they saw that there was a lot less work than the quarter before. This was the direct result of our Trip Scoring Index process, now embedded in our larger strategy. People who had grown accustomed to a hundred hours of pay in a week were only going to be working forty hours. From my office in the other building, I could almost hear the drivers hooting, hollering, screaming, crying. "This is unfair!" "The guy before you told us there was all kinds of money. What did you do with it all?"

I found this reaction amazing. All these people cared about was defending their paycheck. No concern for the service itself or the customers it ostensibly served. Our employees didn't even try to cloak it in the guise of concern for the customer. Just as the Authority had irresponsibly relied on unreliable tax receipts to increase spending, so, too, had many of our employees irresponsibly built their personal finances on historic overtime highs.

"Look," I later said to these guys, when I'd found an opportunity to go to the drivers' room. "Do you really want to defend driving empty buses around? Because I can't defend your driving an empty bus when there is a very real possibility that we aren't going to be able to afford to pay you." I went on: "The purpose of our service is not to serve you. It's to serve our customers. How are we going to explain to fifty thousand people that we had to raise their fares because we were providing inefficient service to five people?"

The day after Labor Day, our "Empty Buses Are Not Good" radio campaign began to run. There was no turning back now. It was the same day the new routes kicked in, with 12 percent less service on the streets. We had identified more than $3 million in service that we found to be unproductive, underutilized, and overly reliant on taxpayer subsidies—far more than the either $1 million or $2 million in service cuts Bob had quietly proposed to the old CEO before I took over. We expected the drivers to picket and protest. We expected the union leadership to call elected officials and tell them how horrible it was. We expected the media to try to fan the flames. We even expected a sharp reaction from our customers.

The first week, the drivers came back and told us horror stories of how the buses were so full they couldn't pick up people who were waiting at the bus stop. The drivers told us that because it was now taking so long to board people, they couldn't possibly keep the buses on time. During the weeks that followed, I made a real effort to spend more time in the drivers' room, listening closely to what people were saying. I wanted to see if there were common themes, and if we needed to make modifications to the major changes we were implementing.

One day around noon, I was in the drivers' room right before the big pullout of buses at one o'clock took place. Joe Libonati, a heavyset driver known around the company as a jokester, told me repeatedly that he was leaving people standing at bus stops every single day. He was so animated in his argument that I asked him where and when he drove. I told him that I wanted to come ride his bus with him to see for myself what he was experiencing.

"Mr. Aesch," he insisted, "it's full. Every single day I'm leaving people standing at the bus stop."

On this day, there was a lot of activity in the drivers' room. People shooting pool, sitting at tables playing cards, and carrying on conversations with one another. Some started to mill around now, as they could see this driver and I were engaged in passionate conversation. "Call me Mark, please," I said. "That's why I'm going to come ride with you. I want to experience what you're experiencing."

"Every single day, I'm telling you," Joe repeated.

"I got it," I said again. "Gonna come ride your bus with you."

Joe paused for a moment. It had started to sink in that I was serious about riding the bus with him. More quietly he said, "Almost every single day my bus is packed full."

"Is that right?" I asked, smiling to myself. "Well I look forward to seeing it with you."

Now he looked worried. "Okay, well, just don't come on Wednesday when you do it. Wednesday's aren't that big a problem, but the other days, it's usually really bad." He smiled sheepishly, realizing that he had surrendered his credibility.

I did go ride the bus one Friday, during a week when he happened to be on vacation. Malcolm Appleberry, the driver on duty, flashed me a big smile as I boarded.

"You have room for me?" I asked.

"Oh, sure," he said.

I stood next to him and surveyed the bus. It was full—a couple people were standing—but not jam-packed.

"Has it been busy this week?" I asked.

He shrugged. "Good loads, but nothing I couldn't handle. You can see for yourself how it is."

It became clear during those first weeks of implementing TSI that the overwhelming majority of driver discontent amounted to unhappiness with the idea of working harder. In some cases we *had* gone too far. We really were leaving people standing at bus stops because we couldn't fit more on board. In those cases, we added service back on. Our Strategic Plan pillar was Putting Buses Where People Wanted to Go, When They Wanted to Go There. That didn't mean simply eliminating service. It meant what it said. And if we needed more equipment, more drivers, and more service to meet that objective, we would provide that.

Over time, our drivers became more accustomed to TSI as well as to the broader strategic concept of Putting Buses Where People Wanted to Go, When They Wanted to Go There. And I could cite any number of other important changes that our employees have accepted, in large part because they now understood clear rationales for the changes. Take spare bus parts. Traditionally, we maintained an in-house department to provide spare parts to our mechanics. In 2004, we issued an RFP for an outside vendor to handle our parts supply. NAPA wound up opening a parts store on our property. At one of our regular employee meetings, I heard horror stories from mechanics about how this would be a disaster. "We won't have the parts we need when we need them," they said. "You have no idea what you're doing!" I listened, but to the mechanics' credit, they gave it a chance. We'd put a great deal of effort into explaining the strategy to them, in this case our Achieve Financial Stability pillar. Over time, the mechanics did come to see that we had a higher percentage of parts available, the parts delivery system was functional for more hours, and we'd taken off our books millions of dollars of inventory that could mysteriously grow legs and disappear in the night.

Perhaps the most gratifying indication I've seen that our efforts to sell in strategy have borne fruit is the tendency of people throughout the organization to work *proactively* now to push our strategic pillars forward. If you just have a command-and-control leader making decisions at will, people will turn into sheep. They'll sit back and let themselves be led. By contrast, RGRTA employees sure are setting forth their own solutions now on a daily basis, and it's pretty amazing to watch.

People in our call center now take the initiative to save money on the copier because they understand what we now call our Long-Term Financial Success pillar and appreciate the challenges facing our organization. Our IT department came up on their own initiative with a plan to do away with individual printers in their offices; they told us specifically that they wanted to help us execute the Long-Term Financial Success pillar. These last two are relatively inconsequential examples, but in my view, radical change occurs in an organization from a thousand small actions taken by empowered employees. And consider the software system we developed in-house for digitally recording all the activity that takes place at accident scenes. We could have gone and spent tons of money on this software, but our employees on their own came back and said, "Rather than buying this, what if we developed it?" We are now considering trademarking and selling the technology, and we've given presentations on it across the country. Not bad for a company that not too long ago was spending its time languidly staring out the window while management took employees on a slow and meandering Sunday afternoon drive, buying drug houses, simulators, and a 1957 bus.

Radical change occurs in an organization from a thousand small actions taken by empowered employees.

Many of our employees weren't in the backseat of the 1969 Malibu ready to go wherever Dad drove. We had a lot of Caesar McFaddens off doing their own thing, not caring or even thinking they had to care. We enjoy sustained success because we've been able to get the guys scrubbing the wheel wells to understand now that they work for the customer rather than the bus.

4.

CHART YOUR ROUTE,
THEN FILL THE TANK

Spend Money Purposely to Support Your Strategy

In ninth grade, when I was on the track team, I really, really wanted a pair of $30 running spikes. One night at dinner, in a thin and faltering voice, I finally worked up the balls to ask my dad. "So I was kind of wondering, what would the chances be that I might be able to get a pair of racing spikes?"

Dad took his enormous, gnarled farmer's hands and reached for his glass of milk. "Your mother just bought you sneakers last year. I don't see what these spike things are going to do any different."

As the uncomfortable silence at our dinner table lingered on, I hoped against hope that my mom would intervene on my behalf. She was as frugal as Dad, but she also had a broader vision of what childhood was supposed to achieve, and it most certainly involved extracurricular activities. My father never understood all the sports, school plays, and the like. To him, they were useless distractions from a single, more important purpose: making money on the farm to assure our survival. His objective was to buy a new hay mower so we could make more bales so we could feed the cows. Nothing impeded that.

My mother did intervene, talking it over with my dad later that night, and I got my running spikes. Fortunately for me, that was the general pattern: My father's single-minded focus on money influenced decisions, but it never overwhelmed my mother's larger vision. I shudder to think what would have happened if it had. I never would have enjoyed formative experiences acting in plays and serving as captain of the cross-country team. I never would have pursued my first career interest as a sports broadcaster doing play-by-play with the school's first video camera.

MOM, DAD, AND BOB FRYE

Our bus company used to live an organizational version of that scenario. We had fallen into the bad habit of putting all decisions through a financial sieve, with Bob Frye and Finance functioning as stand-ins for my dad. As I outlined earlier, Frye came to fill a power vacuum at the top of our organization, effectively taking control of key decisions, even those that had little to do with finance. Sure, senior management plunked down money on a whim to buy 1957 buses. Those were minimal issues involving nominal dollars. But because there was no discernible vision in place, Bob Frye and the Finance Department provided the only legitimate form of guidance there was on all the major issues the organization faced. Unfortunately, that guidance was excessively narrow. Our company wound up directionless and demoralized—like a worn-out 1957 bus puttering around in circles.

It's alarming to think just how much power Finance used to wield. The annual budgeting and capital planning was real simple. The money guys owned the plans. Everybody else followed. End of story. Department heads had a very minimal role in shaping the budget or capital expenditures, just as they had zero authority over salary adjustments. Finance made it clear that they ran the show. If they didn't sign off, it didn't matter whose approval you had—it didn't happen. Frye did send out budget requests to department heads every October, and he even sat down and interviewed department heads to clarify their needs. But that's as far as collaboration went. As one of our executives remembers, "Bob and his staff hammered out a budget and capital plans for the coming year behind closed doors, only consulting with us when they felt the need. We didn't learn about financial decisions until the final budget and capital plans were presented to the board the following February for approval." Even the CEO typically received just a thirty- to sixty-minute briefing on the coming year's budget and capital spending plans. And as far as midyear spending adjustments were concerned, finance simply told department heads that their budgets were being slashed by a given percentage, and that different positions that had been funded or programs that had been supported in the budget had now been removed. Never mind that the department heads might have had different plans for later in the fiscal year. They weren't consulted.

Finance's power went well beyond budgets and capital spending. In Frye's view, every substantial decision the company might face had a financial component; thus every decision fell under his and his team's purview. To ensure we didn't give away too much in the way of salary concessions to our unions, Frye led our labor negotiations, serving as the organization's chief representative at the table. It wasn't even up for debate who would lead negotiations, because money was involved. To make sure we were getting the right people on board, Frye personally made hiring decisions across the organization; it was he, for instance, not our vice president of operations, who hired our director of vehicle maintenance. Frye's department was the judge and jury that articulated the rule of law, as well as the detectives who weeded out instances of what they thought was poor decision-making throughout the organization. Frye himself wore the mantle of arbiter of truth. If he wasn't in the room for a discussion, or if he hadn't weighed in on it, then in his view the conclusions people had reached couldn't be valid, and the analysis couldn't be informed or accurate. Curiously, Finance didn't hold themselves to the same rules they held everybody else to. Even as it ran other departments with an iron fist, Finance added new hires to their own department whenever they wanted, and their departmental operating expenses often came in over budget. The RGRTA's business culture amounted to nothing less than a reign of Finance.

I don't mean to suggest for a minute that Frye himself was power-hungry or on an ego trip. On the contrary, he was genuinely and deeply concerned with the organization's welfare, and he believed that the sound financial decisions he made were in the company's best interests. In truth, he was *forced* to wield so much authority because the organization as a whole lacked vision and the necessary strategies to achieve it. If Bob hadn't stepped in to bring some order, the whole place might well have collapsed. Still, as well-meaning as Frye was, his department wound up functioning in an authoritarian way, and its exercise of power took a severe toll.

You might think that a bit of frustration around the company was okay as long as Frye was making sound financial decisions on the company's behalf. Bob's an extremely smart guy, and his analyses were in fact quite powerful on a purely economic level. Yet it was always more complicated than that. To keep peace inside the organization, Finance had to keep senior leaders happy by funding their pet projects—drug houses, hot dog stands, 1957 buses, and the like. All too often, these spending decisions ate up scarce resources without offering any substantial payback to the organization. In 2002 we started running a daily shuttle in the summertime to Darien Lake, an amusement park located forty miles outside of Rochester. No market research, analysis, or study supported this move. Senior management just announced we'd offer the service, and even though he

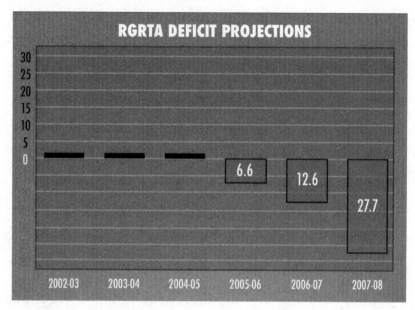

The RGRTA financial condition my first days as CEO.

expected it to fail miserably, Frye complied. The results were as poor as you might expect. Hardly anybody rode the shuttle during the hundred or so days we operated it over two summers, so we wound up discontinuing it after spending tens of thousands of dollars.

Now, lots of companies introduce products that fail. There's nothing wrong with McDonald's introducing pasta into its restaurants, seeing the product flop, and retracting it. But at least McDonald's had a strategy behind the pasta. They had done research, and still the product flopped. Our company couldn't say the same.

To his credit, Frye is the first person today to verify the drawbacks of a reign of Finance. "It wasn't an ideal way of running a business. Today, money is one of the inputs that we look at as we build the broader strategy we're trying to realize. It's much healthier for the company and, Lord knows, for me personally." Yet we don't need to take Frye's word for it, or mine or anyone else's. The numbers speak for themselves.

If you take one thing away from this chapter, make it this: *Financially driven organizations aren't by any means the same as financially successful ones.* I'd bet that our family farm fared better financially with my mom's broader perspective setting the agenda than it would have if my father's strict focus on money had won the day.

Financially driven organizations aren't by any means the same as financially successful ones.

Even during our financial crisis, Bob and his team proved unable to steer the way ahead. Frye's earlier plan to cut $1 million or $2 million in service would have been bloody, bringing with it awful media coverage, layoffs across the board, and internal strife that ultimately would have cost us even more money. By contrast, our strategically driven decision was relatively painless. We removed $3 million of inefficient service with minimal inconvenience to customers and no layoffs thanks to Pete MacNaughton.

PUTTING MONEY WHERE YOUR MOUTH IS

Creating a healthy and productive relationship between Finance and the rest of the organization begins and ends at the top. So often, you see executives abdicating responsibility for pursuing vision. In fact, one of our nation's greatest challenges today is the tendency of elected officials to make inspiring statements during the campaign season and then abandon their agenda upon encountering the stark reality of managing a budget. Staff people begin managing the infrastructure already in place when they take office. Nothing ever improves. Incrementalism reigns. By contrast, if elected officials simply took the vision that they pushed leading up to Election Day, turned that into a governance model, and aligned money beneath that model, we'd all pay much lower taxes and benefit from higher-performing public agencies. Government would become far more dynamic and responsive to changing conditions—much as private companies are compelled to be. We'd avoid bridges to nowhere, fast trains in search of passengers, billion-dollar fighter planes that military officials don't want, and warehouses full of rotting food the government buys to prop up prices.

When I became CEO, there was going to be no doubt at the Authority who was in charge. It was going to be me and our vision, not Finance and Bob Frye. One of the first things we did when I became the RGRTA's CEO was revamp our budgetary process by subordinating it firmly to the strategic development process described in previous chapters. When we do finally connect the financial process to strategy development, Frye and his team still do much of the work. But they aren't standing there with their hands on the guillotine, ready to strike. Rather, they meet with each department head to evaluate his or her views, just like I meet with our FLAG team. Finance is then *required* to present to the entire executive management team, including me, a bottom line summary of all the department head requests, with no judgment from Finance as to the viability of these requests. Finance goes on to provide some interpretation as to what they believe makes sense, as well as a recommendation for the Financial Plan. Our executive management team then spends a month in heated debate about how to ensure that the Financial Plan invests in the already agreed upon Strategic Plan and Operating Plan. Following this, the entire process is opened up once again to department heads; no more waiting for the board to get it before they see what's in the plan.

The department heads are given one week to appeal our budgetary decisions. If a manager feels passionately that an important request of hers hasn't made it through our attempt to connect the Financial and Operating Plans, that manager can sit down with executive management and talk it out. These past couple of years alone, we added multiple staff positions in IT and Grants Administration, as well as a number of safety-related initiatives in the maintenance area, because department heads took advantage of the appeals process. Ryan Gallivan, newly promoted to vice president of Lift Line and regional operations as a result of his participation in our Trip Scoring process, wound up getting that new part-time bus washer that he wanted to hire. "It's a more balanced, rational approach," he observes. "Money is important, but it isn't everything. Now the department heads have a chance to be heard, and the company benefits."

After appeals have been exercised, we share the completed plan with our entire administrative workforce and give them a period of time to comment and react to the draft plan. Only after we've incorporated their reactions do we present our Comprehensive Plan— containing the Strategic, Operating, and Financial Plans—to our board for adoption.

Our process as a whole ensures that all ideas are properly vetted. Bureaucrats don't call the shots, and neither do bosses. No way could a 1957 bus or a Darien Lake amusement park shuttle fall through the cracks. Whether I come up with an idea or a recep-

Bureaucrats don't call the shots, and neither do bosses.

tionist does, the ideas are each evaluated, scored, and funded (or not) based on collective judgments about how well the idea helps us realize our vision. Our chairman, John Doyle, explains: "If there's anything we've done differently around here, it's strategy development. This has us moving in a straight line and adopting policies that make sense. When we put dollars behind an initiative, we can feel secure because we don't spend money on good ideas; we spend it on ideas that take us where we're trying to go."

We've also altered how we go about our capital planning. Department heads connect every single request they make for capital funds to a strategic pillar, explaining how the expenditure will help to advance or achieve that pillar. A cross-functional team of mid-level people then evaluates each request based on the anticipated ROI to the company (the financial sieve), balanced with the ability of the proposed expenditure to advance the strategy. We're bringing both Mom *and* Dad's opinion to the table when an employee asks for something. That mid-level team then makes their recommendations, which go to executive management for final evaluation and incorporation into the capital plan. Today, our Finance Department can cite many projects that they wouldn't have funded under our old "Finance decides everything" system, but that have been awarded funding because of the rating they received from our team of mid-level employees. These projects include a bus lift for our oversized sixty-foot buses, a software upgrade for our accident reporting technology, repairs to the sprinkler system in our Operations Building, an upgrade to the electrical system in our maintenance area, installation of new tire-changing equipment, and replacement of two steam cleaners to wash the floors of our garages.

I've described how finance links the budget up with a strategic development process already in progress, but I need to emphasize: The annual strategic planning reigns supreme. It's the most important thing that I do as CEO every year. I personally invest hundreds of hours in the development of our plan. Although we incorporate so many inputs from so many sources, at the end of the day it is clear that the plan is our plan—and decidedly not Finance's.

It's interesting: As much as our board embraces, applauds, and appreciates the time and energy we spend on strategy, several members have suggested that we scale back our effort. It seems to take up so much of management's bandwidth; maybe there's an easier way, they suggest. We appreciate this perspective, but we reject it. As we see it, the concerted effort we make in developing a plan rooted in strategy is what keeps our organization honest and prevents a relapse into rule-by-Finance. The process of writing our Comprehensive Plan is valuable in and of itself because it forces strategy-based decisions. Again and again, we hire senior executives, fire senior

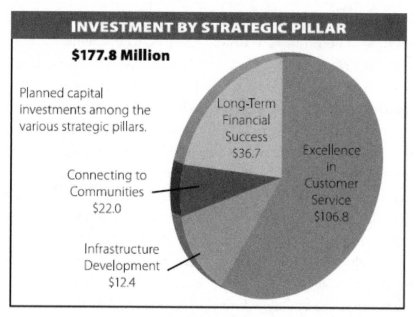

Matching money to our stategies.

executives, demote department heads, promote mid-level employees, alter strategies, change our planned capital expenditures, and react to new construction and business—all as a direct result of this sophisticated process.

TIDE . . . IT'S MORE THAN JUST CLEAN UNIFORMS!

Several years ago, we developed a $25 million program called Technology Initiatives for Driving Excellence (TIDE). The program encompassed twenty-eight different technology projects—things like a GPS radio communications system for our fleet of buses, a state-of-the-art fleet maintenance information system, a yard management software program for buses on our campus, and a next-bus technology system to tell customers in their bus shelter precisely when their bus will be there. TIDE was the largest capital project ever undertaken in our organization's history, and we added a significant number of staff to manage it inside our organization rather than hiring external consultants at multiple times the cost. As we were developing our Comprehensive Plan for 2010, we identified nearly seventy-five new administrative positions that we thought the organization should fund. Those seventy-five included a dozen or so people specifically hired to help us take full advantage of all of the ongoing maintenance and operation of TIDE, as well as analysis of the data flowing through it. Just as we were connecting our Operating and Financial Plans for the coming year, it became clear to us that we were likely to see a multimillion-dollar reduction in state aid for the coming year. We faced a difficult question: What should we do?

Much as we had done years earlier when presenting our initial Comprehensive Plan, senior management sat down with our board at a governance retreat to preview our plan. I got up and described the strategy development process we had taken the company through over the prior six months. I then laid out three possible doors we could open. The first door was to keep fares stable, protect the status quo (i.e., don't hire the seventy-five people), continue the capital investment in TIDE, and use only a small amount of the money we kept in our piggy bank to balance our budget. The second door was to keep fares stable for a short period, hire some but not all of the new staff we wanted, continue with our TIDE initiative, but use much of our cash reserves in the next couple of years. The third was to hire all seventy-five people that our planning process had identified, raise fares in short order, and severely jeopardize our financial future.

The board asked some tough questions. "Have you thought about what fuel might do going forward?" "Are you convinced that the state is only going to cut aid by 5 percent a year and not more?" "Have you funded the likely growth in health care expenses over the next three years?" "What happens if the union contract in negotiation winds up supporting the union's position rather than management's position?"

After much debate, almost all of us agreed that we should build a plan for the coming year around what we called our "door and a third" strategy. That is, we'd keep fares stable, invest fully in the TIDE initiative so as to complete it, and hire the adequate staffing to optimize those technologies, but not the other administrative employees. This meant that we'd hire a database administrator, but not a Lift Line road supervisor. We'd hire a software engineer, but not a communications person. Strategy would drive the decisions as to what would be funded and what wouldn't be.

Energized by this decision, our leadership team went away and around that strategy built a revised plan for the coming year. Through December and the holidays, we engaged in lengthy conference calls and rigorous debate over which operating tactics identified through our staff-driven process we'd adopt and which of the seventy-five positions we had identified it would be most helpful to have. Over the course of no less than sixteen meetings, we tried to determine which specific measures would meet the board-certified strategy of keeping fares stable and optimizing technologies. "This was really hard," remembers Hal Carter, our general counsel. "We had gone through a tough planning process and had laid out a clear strategy with solid operating tactics, and now we had to go back and revisit it. People were arguing about whether a particular job helped to advance TIDE more than a budget analyst might help us make smarter financial decisions. The fact is we needed both; we'd already established that. We sure did go through a lot of boxes of donuts that month." Chris Dobson, our budget manager, chimes in, "And I'd like to point out that Finance purchased those donuts! But seriously, as long and as painful as those sessions were, it was the most informed we had ever been in spending money."

HOW REINING IN FINANCE WON US A
CULTURE-CHANGING UNION DEAL

From the start, I anticipated rough times ahead with our union. Our contract was set to expire on December 31, 2006, and we would need to negotiate a new one. Six months before the expiration date, Debbie convened a team of people who'd participate in negotiations both at the table and behind the scenes. She also shared with the union leadership our offer to resolve the contract. Knowing that union leadership regularly misled the workforce, we shared it with all the rank-and-file employees, too. Employees were astonished at how generous our offer was—an almost 17 percent salary increase over five years. In putting that kind of money on the table (the last time there had been contract negotiations, management had offered just 6 percent over a three-year period), we sought something in return: changes in work rules and other concessions we believed would help us operate more efficiently and transform our workplace environment in support of our strategic pillars. Tactically, we intended to take advantage of the fact that there were three times as many bus drivers in the union as mechanics; bus drivers didn't care so much about burdensome work rules in the maintenance area that we wanted to change, and so would put up less resistance. Also, if labor arbitrators arrived at what we believed to be inappropriate decisions, we intended to litigate those cases, forcing the union leadership to spend money we knew they could ill afford.

As they always did, union leadership didn't take negotiations seriously and frittered time away. Over a period of about two years, we faced protests, pickets, and personal attacks on both Debbie and myself. They threatened to disrupt a family Fourth of July picnic at my house. They casually mentioned that they knew where Debbie's children went to school. They wrote obnoxious or obscene gossip on the Internet. Yet still we didn't waver in support of our negotiating plan.

During this period, Bob Frye was strident in his opposition to our bargaining position. We had already agreed that our strategy was going to be about culture change, but meeting after meeting he kept trying to undo our decision and make the union negotiations about money. "You're giving away the farm," he said. "This whole thing could and should be settled for far less. And what are we getting in return? A couple less sick days per employee?" I tried to convince Bob that we were seeking to achieve a greater purpose, that this wasn't just about the cheapest contract, but I don't think he fully understood that at the time. Bob had accepted and even embraced his absence at the negotiating table, but he still wanted his *philosophy* represented at the table.

In truth, we hoped to get far more than a couple fewer sick days. Our proposal would require all employees to participate in the cost of health care, helping us get them to appreciate that this was a benefit that cost real money. Under our old contract, employees could not show up for work for eighteen days a year, above and beyond their scheduled vacation days. Our new proposal would reduce that to eleven days, allowing us to decrease the number of situations in which we were counting on an employee to drive a bus, do a brake job, or clean a bus, and he or she didn't show up. We also proposed to eliminate craft severance, whereby a mechanic in one section of the garage had to stop working until an "authorized" mechanic from a completely separate side of the garage could arrive to perform the most basic of functions. Another arcane rule—the "layoff book," whereby the first two people who signed into a book every day could take the day off, whether they had any time coming to them or not—would also bite the dust. We increased probation time for new employees from twelve to thirty-nine weeks and proposed a system of performance incentives that would allow us to reward employees for hitting certain performance goals. All told, these rules would turbocharge our operations while also nurturing the culture of no ego and helping to implant an ethic of accountability throughout the organization (discussed in the next chapter).

Our union negotiations function like baseball arbitration: In the event an agreement can't be reached, both sides submit a last best offer and an arbitrator picks one or the other. There is no splitting the baby; one side wins, and the other loses. In December 2008, the day of reckoning arrived. We held a meeting to determine what our final offer would be. It was time to put our money where our mouth was. Were we going to hold firm to our strategy? Or would we give in to Bob Frye's dollars-and-cents logic? It was a difficult call. We were putting a lot of money on the table, and I couldn't be sure that we would really see the payback we were hoping for. Debbie and I were clear about wanting cultural change so that the top supervisors would be freed up to better manage their departments on a day-by-day, hour-by-hour basis. In the end, we resolved that if we were going to have our offer selected, we wanted it to be one we would be proud to implement, and that meant culture change. We stayed true to the strategy we had adopted back in 2006.

We were in for a surprise. In a nearly unprecedented move, the international vice president of the transit union became involved in our negotiations, and we were able to reach an agreement in short order without going to arbitration. In November 2009, the employees went over to their union hall to vote on whether to ratify the agreement. We were nervous. Local union leadership was still vehement in its opposition. During the course of the day, though, I ran into a couple of drivers who flashed me thumbs-up signs. Around six thirty that night, we got the good news: The employees had passed the agreement by a four-to-one margin. With the exception of performance incentives, we got all the elements of our final proposal. And to put the cherry on top, our local union was placed into trusteeship by the international, and all the thuggish local leadership was removed. Remember how union leadership ripped up that piece of paper when we asked for their cooperation to help us deal with our financial crisis? You could almost hear that paper being taped back together again, with enormous opportunities for labor, management, the organization, our customers, and taxpayers.

SWIMMING IN HIS LANE

Year in and year out, Bob has not only accepted a reduction in Finance's power but eagerly participated in our more collaborative budgeting and capital expenditures processes. He's engaged in fruitful discussions about strategy and supported my efforts to put it front and center in our organization. He's clearly been a major reason for our success rather than the impediment to it that I'd first feared he might be. When it came to the union negotiations, Bob simply disagreed with our strategy; he didn't reject the notion that we should have a strategy, or believe that he should be the sole arbiter of it.

Once he saw that operating according to a strategy would make us even more successful than a dictatorship of Finance had, it was a done deal: He was fully committed. Bob would be less powerful, but the expenditure of money would be more purposeful. Bob wanted organizational success, not personal success, and he wound up enjoying both. In 2004, when I had finally decided to keep him on, I had cut his staff, reduced his salary, and moved his office. Since then, the new Bob Frye has seen his staff grow again, his pay increase, and his office move back to its original location.

Bob Frye's transformation symbolizes that of our entire company. Here was someone who used to think he deserved a $700 office chair now taking that chair outside the room at union negotiations. Here was someone who used to dictate to department heads what their budgets would be now engaging in productive, consultative discussions. Here was someone who used to appoint himself as auditor of other departments' daily operations now reporting on how Finance was working to stay within budget and authorizing hiring limits. Today, Bob is respected rather than feared. And he's happier for it, too.

When Finance controlled everything, our financial performance was abysmal, but now that Finance plays a role, our finances have gone through the roof. As for the organization, we've already mentioned our wide-ranging turnaround from deficit to surplus. And all this at a time when school districts, water authorities, public safety organizations, cities, counties, and entire states around the country are bleeding cash and begging for handouts.

Change really can happen—in individuals as well as organizations. People can learn to do things differently. Bob and I talk about these things from time to time as we take long drives to Albany, our state capitol, along the New York State Thruway. I haven't hugged Bob in a hotel lobby yet with tears in my eyes, but I hope that he realizes just how proud of him I am. He's swimming in his own lane now, and his performance has earned our team a gold medal.

5.

TO AVOID GETTING A TICKET, WATCH YOUR OWN SPEEDOMETER

Embrace Accountability in All That You Do

On the farm, I received an allowance of three dollars a week. Lots of kids get allowances for things like vacuuming, taking out the garbage, and cleaning up their room. I had to do these things in exchange for the three dollars my dad paid me, but I also had to throw down bales of hay to the barn floor from our haymow, climb the ladder to the top of our two silos and throw down ground-up corn for the cows to eat, sweep the mangers where the cows ate the corn and hay, let the cows out of the barn in the morning and put them back in at night, feed them, and of course, my personal favorite, lug out wheelbarrows full of cow shit and push them up a ramp to the machine that spread it across the fields. Did I mention I got to do this in *two* barns? And feed the dogs, cats, turkey, rabbits, chickens, pony, and ducks. Twice a day, seven days a week! For three dollars.

Realizing that my allowance was not enough to keep me motivated, my dad created incentive opportunities. One summer, we hired a group of guys to replace the roof on our main barn. The workmen did a good job, but they dropped hundreds of stray nails everywhere. This was a real problem. On a farm, stray nails will puncture the tires of farm equipment. We also ran the risk of cows stepping on the nails and injuring themselves, which would lead to serious vet bills. Not to mention the danger to us kids running around in bare feet! But by this point, you know my dad pretty well; the cows and farm equipment were his top priority.

One Sunday morning over pancakes, my dad made an announcement: He would pay us a penny for each nail we found near the barn. Awesome, I thought. Since I was making about nine cents an hour for doing my barn chores, a penny for each nail I picked up was enough to get my attention. My brother had the same reaction. So did my mom and my sisters. We were all highly motivated in the weeks that followed to pick up nails. I can imagine what it was like at Sutter's Mill back in 1849; we treated these nails like gold. Our cousins, aunts, and uncles would come over to visit for the express purpose of looking for nails. One day, my cousin Joel and I hit the motherload. We had squeezed into a tight space between two tall silos where we kept ground-up corn feed. This was a place where farm equipment or cows couldn't go. Nails here had fallen on the ground an inch thick. I think I paid for my first year of college that day.

My dad had designed an incentive system that got his people to focus on what he needed to achieve. Paying a penny a nail, even if that meant spending a hundred dollars over the course of the summer, was far less than what he would have had to spend on fixing farm equipment or mending cows' hooves. What my dad might not have realized was that having an incentive program in place also had a second helpful effect. It caused us to feel more responsible for our own performance. Since we got paid more for finding more nails, we now had a way of understanding how well we had done on a task day in and day out. Turning in our cupfuls of nails each evening to my dad, we came to internalize a drive to monitor and report on our own performance. We took pride in doing better and better each day and even came to compete against one another to become the best nail picker-uppers we could be.

Inspired by my dad, our company has nurtured a culture of accountability by creating an elaborate salary system that incentivizes people to perform well, and that in the process trains them to become aware of performance levels at any given point in time. Some companies just hand out fixed bonuses each year pegged to a measure of overall company performance, such as stock price. This would be the equivalent of my dad paying out a premium based on how much we sold the cows for at the end of the year. The measurements we select to pay incentives, by contrast, are connected to much more specific goals that relate to our strategic objectives—the equivalent to how many nails we pick up each day. We don't pay out incentives for their own sake, but because we want to hold people accountable—and encourage them to hold themselves accountable—for solid performance that benefits the organization.

We also go further and design our review process for senior executives so that their efforts to reach strategic goals will trickle down to others below them in the organization. Sixty days before our department heads receive their reviews, they learn of their incentives for the coming fiscal year. They also are provided with a pot of money to dispense to their subordinates. A smart department head will build an incentive compensation program for their own employees consistent with how I am going to construct the department head's. The result is an organization where everyone from top to bottom feels a sense of accountability for performance in alignment with strategy.

As our director of operations, Bruce Philpott oversees our main fleet of buses on the road every day. He learns that he'll have an incentive tied to the on-time performance of our buses, in order to help us realize our pillar of Excellence in Customer Service. Bruce in turn very wisely constructs incentive opportunities for his staff of reports—the radio controllers and road supervisors on the street—tied to reducing the percentage of buses that are early (which is bad), since a lower early percentage will improve his overall scores. Each of

Bruce's reports receives $500 extra each quarter if the percentage of early buses is brought below 5.5 percent.

Joe Jablonski, our new director of vehicle maintenance, has an incentive now related to hitting our goal of .40 missed trips daily. We define a missed trip as an occasion when we lack the number of buses necessary to drive one off the property at the scheduled time to pick up customers. Reducing missed trips also supports our Excellence in Customer Service pillar. In 2008–2009, we missed our goals in this area quarter after quarter. Our goal was .35 per day and we averaged more than .73. An abject failure. We weren't even close. I told Joe that we'd keep this incentive in place for him the coming fiscal year, 2009–2010. We made the goal a little bit easier, .50. Joe very wisely built a new incentive compensation program for all his garage foremen related to the percentage of buses available to be called into service at any point in the day. As a result, both the garage foremen and Joe hit their missed-trips goals in every quarter of 2009. In fact they even beat the more challenging goal they'd had the earlier year: .29 in the first quarter, then .17, .28, and finally .26 in the last quarter. "Pretty cool that we get more for meeting our numbers," says Pete Gottschalk, a garage foreman. "Now we're thinking more about what we're doing. It's in our brains."

At first, our incentive program didn't work so well because we'd underfunded it. Now mid-level managers can make 3 to 10 percent more each year if they hit their numbers—not a bad boost for helping the company succeed. We've also increased the number of employees eligible for incentives, spreading the program throughout the company. In recent years, all of our regional bus operators, of which there are nearly 150, have participated in our incentive compensation program. This past year, a group of mid-level Teamsters Union supervisors at our largest subsidiary elected to participate. The lone holdout continues to be the employees represented by the infamous union leadership of "we ain't giving nothing back." These dinosaurs actually leave money for their members on the table. Their members are still answerable for things like on-time performance, the announcing of stops, and bus cleanliness; yet they don't enjoy the financial rewards that otherwise would accrue to them for putting up strong numbers. The union bosses' unspoken argument is indefensible: Management should receive financial reward for hitting numbers, yet the line employees who clean the buses, ensure they don't break down, and help them arrive on time should do without. Glad I don't have to defend *that* line of reasoning.

In our business, when a bus breaks down on the road, it's called a disabled bus. In 2005, when we were building our first measurement device, our Customer Satisfaction Index, one of the measurement areas was the average number of disabled buses on a daily basis. Agreeing on the goal—an average of one broken-down bus per day—was easy. Agreeing on the definition of a disabled bus was not. We attempted to do this in the working group we had established to build the index, but it became clear that we needed a much more sophisticated definition than we had first thought, so the discussion moved to a leadership team meeting. It was a meatier topic than the sorts of things we used to talk about, like the color of bus stop sign poles.

We began by batting around a number of questions. Is the bus disabled when the driver calls in and says that he can't drive it anymore? Is it disabled when the radio controller classifies it as disabled? Is it disabled if there are no customers on board? If it's at the end of the route? If a replacement bus gets there within fifteen minutes? Is it disabled if a bus gets there before the next regularly scheduled bus would pass through this location?

After thirty minutes, it was clear we'd gotten no closer to a resolution. So we scheduled a portion of the leadership team to meet again the next Friday. In the intervening week, Ann Nichols and Jerry Siconolfi spent time on their own, debating scenarios that would classify a bus as "disabled." It might sound strange that we were spending all this time trying to figure out how to define a broken-down bus, but if you're going to have true accountability, you need stark, precise agreement as to what an employee—and in this case an entire organization—is being held accountable for.

During the follow-up meeting, the larger group gathered again to work in more depth through this definition. We spent two hours that morning walking ourselves down every angle of what it meant for a bus to be disabled, before we finally reached the conclusion. Jerry Siconolfi argued that so long as he was able to repair or replace the bus before the next scheduled bus was due to pass through the route, then it shouldn't count as disabled. We wound up throwing out that definition, preferring one that spoke to the actual customer experience of being on a disabled bus. A bus might not be scheduled to pass through for another half an hour. If a repaired bus arrived in twenty-eight minutes, a customer on the original, broken-down bus would certainly experience displeasure with the service and wish us to consider that bus "disabled." Our final definition of a disabled bus, then, was the following: any bus that is unable to complete its journey with customers on board and that we cannot replace with another bus within five minutes.

If the definitions underlying our incentive program are strict, so, too, is our adherence to the program's goals. In 2005–2006, several of us, including myself, plugged away at an incentive related to ridership growth. Ridership had been sluggish or declining at the Authority for years, and I had a $2,400 incentive riding on our ability to achieve 1 percent growth. While ridership did grow, we missed our goal by a few tenths of a percent. We all left several thousand dollars on the table because in our organization, close doesn't cut it.

Of course, you'll always have some people who think that close does cut it. In 2006, Jerry Siconolfi had come up just short on several different incentive opportunities. He made an impassioned plea to Debbie Griffith and me that we round up his results. It was a Tuesday morning when they both came to consult me on the issue. "Look," Jerry said, "we all broke our asses to reduce the number of buses that broke down on the street. It's supposed to be one a day. What'd I get, a one point one? Can't we just call it a one? I mean, let's be real. It's going to be hard for me to keep people motivated if we don't pay. I was really counting on this."

Debbie shook her head. "Jerry, for the one-tenth of a percent of the customers who had the buses break down on them, one point one did not equal a one. If we're going to maintain the integrity of our incentive program, this can't just be a cash grab."

I nodded in agreement. "Look, Jerry, it's great that we've seen improvement in this area. I don't mean to diminish that. But you're going to have to figure out how to motivate your employees to do even better."

Jerry spent a while longer trying to convince Debbie and me to bend, but we wouldn't have it. Finally, he heaved a big sigh and got up to go. "I'm just really disappointed. I feel like I give this place my all. I really think we should recognize the great improvement we've made in maintenance."

We had seen improvement. Yet Jerry wanted us to agree that one point one really was a one. And as far as our organization is concerned, it's not. Either you have a system that holds people accountable for performance, or you don't. There is no middle ground, because the minute you start believing that there is, you begin to erode the culture of accountability.

Incentive compensation can't be perceived as, nor in reality be, simply a mechanism for higher salary. If you feel that way, then just pay people more money. The whole point of our incentive compensation program is to connect with actual results related to strategy. Any cooking of the books or rounding up does not equal actual results. Ask the Enrons and Adelphias of the world if it's okay to "round up" when they report their quarterly earnings to Wall Street. In our case, we have to be especially vigilant about integrity so as not to fall back on our old culture, in which accountability wasn't a value internalized among our workforce, but a power exercised by Finance.

Our chairman, John Doyle, played an instrumental role in helping us understand the importance of incentives, especially when it
came to senior management. Although our company excels in its
performance, we don't pay any higher salary to our senior management on that basis. Rather, we set base salaries by looking at what
executives at other companies like ours make. If we at the top want to
earn above-market money, we have to attain predetermined strategic
goals and cash in on incentives. There's no shortcut and no giveaways.

Another way we ensure the absolute integrity of our system of
accountability is by making sure that the data is solid. Many big
companies with incentive structures don't have to worry so much
about the quality of data because their incentive opportunities are
largely tied to broad-brush financial targets like stock price or improvement in margins. When you start tying incentives to precise
strategic objectives, as I argue companies should, the legitimacy of data
becomes a serious issue. Our goal may be to encourage self-regulation
among our workforce, yet there are limits to what self-reporting can
accomplish. In order to advance accountability, we make sure to
verify the self-reported results on which we base our incentive
awards. Our entire measurement system, which we'll discuss more
in the next chapter, uses inputs either from technology or outside
vendors. We maintain a secret-shopper program to check on our
customer experience and a company-wide program to evaluate
quantitatively how well our people interact on the phone. At the
end of the year, we have an outside auditor inspect the integrity of
the entire system. "You've got to be strict," Doyle notes. "We pay
out hundreds of thousands of dollars each year to reward good
performance. Nothing is paid until the board learns about the
results and accepts them. It's a tight program that hinges on the
truth facing."

IF YOU WANT THE GOODIES,
DELIVER THE GOODS

Incentives represent the positive side of our efforts to create an orga-nization of accountability. The negative side is a tightening of the screws on any practice or behavior inconsistent with that goal. One huge way we've cracked down on irresponsible behavior is by tight-ening up our workers' compensation practices. Our old method for awarding workers' compensation was downright scandalous. All a worker needed to do was indicate that he or she was injured on the job, and our staff would encourage that individual to file for workers' compensation and coach him or her through the process. Not only was there no process built in to detect fraud, our staff routinely *facilitated* fraud. Say a driver had injured his shoulder painting his house over the weekend. He'd casually mention to a longtime em-ployee in Human Resources that this off-premises incident had happened. The HR person would bend the rules and help the driver fill out the proper paperwork, making it appear the employee had . gotten injured steering the bus, even though the HR person knew full well that the employee wasn't entitled to benefits. As part of the scam, the HR person would take all the paperwork and turn it over to the outside vendor who managed the program for us. Then we would start writing checks. Neither the outside vendor nor our own employees were vested in pursuing our organization's interests.

Since we had no case management, people could go out on compensation for months with no contact from our organization. Our organization lost hundreds of thousands of dollars a year, not to mention the lost labor of a trained professional employee. And each year, it was getting worse. In 2004, we were paying out more than $3.5 million a year in workers' compensation.

In 2006, with our financial crisis in control, we finally fixed the system. We wanted employees who really were injured on the job to get compensation, while also ensuring that we could maximize their benefits by cutting down on fraudulent claims. So we brought management of the program in-house. Now our Legal Department owns this process, supported by Finance. One of our employees, Julie Tennant, actively manages every case every week. She knows every case by name, by the date it went into the system, and by its current status. Her personal investment is phenomenal. We also have private investigators who go out and interact with employees who are committing fraud. We aggressively prosecute and require repayment. We have even charged people with and convicted them of felonies.

The first ex-employee we convicted, a former bus driver, had gone on disability way back in 1992, complaining of back pains. By the mid 2000s, he'd been receiving workers' compensation checks from the Authority for thirteen years. One of our in-house attorneys, Amy Coté, wondered how this man could have lived for so long on a weekly check of less than $200 from us, so she ordered an investigation. It turned out that our apparently injured ex-employee was quite active indeed roofing houses for a living. A private investigator hired to follow this guy found him driving an old pickup truck with ladders attached to the back bed. The ex-employee stopped to pick up another man, and the two of them made their way into a nice neighborhood, where our ex-employee was then spotted climbing up a house and nailing shingles onto a roof. We later got affadavits from nine families stating that they'd hired our ex-employee to repair or install their roofs. In 2007, we got our ex-employee convicted of fraud, an offense for which he served five weeks in jail. We tried to recover our workers' compensation payments, but to no avail: Our ex-employee has successfully filed for poor person's status.

Even without reimbursement in this and other cases, our workers' compensation expenses have dropped by millions. By 2009, we had cut our $3.5 million a year to less than $2.1 million—a nearly 60 percent reduction. In 2009 alone, workers' compensation expenses fell by $500,000, a 21 percent reduction. By that time our workers' compensation reserves (a fund for future expenses we think we're likely to incur but haven't paid yet) was down more than $800,000, a 15 percent reduction. Total workers' compensation payments were down $450,000, a reduction of 25 percent. In relating these results, I should emphasize that we don't ever want Julie Tennant to keep the number of claims below a certain level. In that case, we would be wrongly motivating Julie to deny workers' compensation to employees who deserve it. We'd be unable to see if a systematic problem at our company was causing worker injuries. We measure and reward Julie's success in other ways, such as evaluating the training programs she runs, the extent to which she has improved workplace safety, and her ability to settle old, long-term claims left over from years gone by.

Beyond tightening up specific programs, we've signaled that accountability matters by removing employees who have failed to conduct themselves in a responsible way on the job. For many years, we employed a liability claims manager to handle claims filed with our company by accident victims. When an accident occurs on public transportation, the biggest struggle we face is dealing with all those people in the neighborhood who race to get on the bus so that they can file false accident claims. Unfortunately for us, it was our liability claims manager who did the dealing. To many of us, this person seemed to embody the spirit of a militant unionized staff person who didn't view the Authority's money as a finite resource. With no approval and no authority, all people had to do was call her, say they were a customer, say they had been on a certain bus, and she would mail them Wal-Mart gift cards as compensation. Unfortunately, our claims manager wouldn't require a release document from them in return, so these people would sue us anyway. Incredible.

This longtime employee enjoyed complete autonomy; she could serve as the intake valve for a claim, conclude something about the merits of the claim, and then walk from her office to accounting and request payment, with no oversight from the legal department at all. Even finance wasn't watching her. Not surprisingly, the claims manager was good friends with the woman in Human Resources who was advising our employees on how to fill out workers' compensation claims for things like painting their houses. No accident that neither of them celebrated when we succeeded or left dejected when we failed. Our claims manager liked to ride in the back of the wagon, watching her colleagues out front pulling on the tongue, slogging through the mud. Her meter never moved; she wasn't concerned about monitoring her own performance and improving it to the extent she could. She came to work each week to get five days closer to retirement. Her total lack of concern for organizational success was unacceptable, and soon after I became CEO we invited her to retire, which I'm happy to report she did. The HR woman who juiced the workers' compensation claims was thanked for her work around the same time.

ACCOUNTABILITY AT THE TOP

I personally try to model a spirit of accountability in a couple of ways. First, as the chief representative of our organization to the outside world, I look for as many opportunities as I can to invite outsiders to hold us accountable for our organizational performance. An important vehicle for this is our annual Comprehensive Plan, published in a bound edition with an opening letter from me and our chairman. In each one of our key strategic areas, at the beginning of that section of the plan we specifically state that "On March 31 of the following year,* the Authority will have been successful if the following has occurred." We typically list five to eight results that we expect to achieve, accompanied by specific numbers for each strategic pillar. We also broadcast who in our organization is accountable for specific tactics. And in rehashing our perfor-

---

*Our fiscal year runs April 1 through March 31.

mance for the previous year, we acknowledge when we have failed to meet our own, self-generated performance goals.

People I meet remark how astonished they are that our Comprehensive Plan is not merely a cheerleading document in disguise. They also note that I don't play the CEO's usual cheerleader role in my personal appearances. I remember during my first year as CEO doing a couple of live interviews with Kristin Miranda, a news reporter for a local TV station. I came in at 5:30 A.M. that day, and after doing a live cut-in at 6:10, we spent a pleasant few minutes talking about the value of public transportation while sitting in a bus parked on our lot. I explained to Kristin how bad we were at cleaning the buses. I got up and showed her ground-in grime in the corners of the floor, the dried soda spills and the gunk that had hardened over time under the seats in the back of the bus. "Wow," she said, "it's so refreshing to hear a CEO acknowledge that their organization is actually bad at something. You typically only hear that everything is great."

Another way I hold myself accountable on behalf of the organization is with our Customer Town Meetings. I first got the idea for town meetings while serving as an aide for U.S. Representative Bill Paxon. Bill was a tremendous elected official. Every month he would hold town meetings across his nine-county district, talking with and listening to the people whom he represented. These events could become tedious and monotonous, but every month he insisted on doing them. Coffee shops, farmers' barns, small businesses, and fire halls were all venues for the Paxon town meeting tour. And because we would always do them on Saturdays, when local media was starved for something to cover, we routinely received precious news coverage.

I still remember watching the local news one Saturday night when the media had come out to a farm to interview Bill on some national issue. The anchor read copy into Bill's sound bite, saying, "Bill Paxon held *another* of his town meetings today . . ." Music to our ears. We had ingrained in their minds the notion that Bill *always* held town meetings. Victory! Not coincidentally, Bill won elections by large margins.

As CEO I resolved to replicate Paxon's process, and within ninety days of my appointment we held our first Customer Town Meeting. As it turned out, we didn't learn much that we didn't already know, but our customers saw that we were listening and our senior level managers realized that this whole "paying attention to the customer thing" wasn't just empty words on a bumper sticker. Even after that meeting, I think some of our managers continued to suspect that I would roll out this entire program and then content myself with letting other people do the work. They were wrong; unless I have a last-minute conflict I can't resolve, I still conduct town meetings myself. As leader of our organization, I think it's important that our entire organization, and I as its representative, take this opportunity to show accountability before our customers.

Customer Town Meetings are great, but as a representative of RGRTA, I've also tried to get other transit systems across the country to help us evaluate our performance. The reason it was so special when Red Sox great Ted Williams batted .406 was because nobody else had done so. You never know if you're any good unless you can compare yourself against others. Airplanes are on schedule about 76 percent of the time. Several years ago, our on-time performance was exactly the same. After a lot of work, our buses now arrive on schedule 84 percent of the time. But it would be even more valuable if we could compare our performance with other mid-sized bus companies. I've tried on three different occasions in recent years to build a benchmarking group of similar sized transit systems. The first two times, I couldn't generate any interest. But now I believe we've got a fighting

You never know if you're any good unless you can compare yourself against others.

chance to collaborate with five other systems, sharing and comparing data on half a dozen different areas of measurement, such as on-time performance, revenue per mile, and so on. Most any objective analysis would say that our performance is very high in Rochester, yet we're always seeking out still another evaluation tool to hold ourselves as an organization more accountable.

Beyond benchmarking, we've sought to seed our entire industry and beyond with a spirit of accountability. For years, state bureaucrats have defended a "needs-based" distribution model, whereby the system that "needed more" got more. This invited chronic underperformance as transit systems purposely placed themselves in the position of needing more, with absolutely no concern for accountability. We took this perverse system and turned it on its head, working with state legislators to introduce performance-based state aid legislation. As of this writing, we've had the legislation formally introduced, and we continue to fight for its passage. If we succeed, we will revolutionize government agencies in New York State. Imagine if every school district, transit system, and sewer department got money according to how well it did. All of a sudden, the entire government sector, which represents about 25 percent of the New York State economy, would start to work better. And imagine if this happened nationwide, where government spending represents around 40 percent or more of the total economy.*

A second way I've tried to model accountability within our organization is to hold myself responsible for my own work performance to the best of my ability. My annual performance review has been an important starting point. Years earlier, the CEO's annual review process centered around one topic: How much more would

---

*Usgovernmentspending.com, accessed April 4, 2010, puts government spending at 45 percent of GDP. A slightly lower estimate of 38 percent is provided at http://www.cato-at-liberty.org/2009/12/10/government-and-gdp/.

they pay him next year? That was determined by the full board in one meeting. While performance reviews existed for other employees, the CEO position had been exempt. No review process existed. No analysis. No benchmarking. Compare that to today, where there's an exhaustive review process. I invest more than a dozen hours completing an eight-page self-evaluation of my performance of the year before. I then offer the executive management team time to comment on my self-evaluation before we turn it over to the board. After the board has had the chance to see my evaluation, they each take the time to provide comments, which are consolidated in my formal review, conducted by the chairman. Compensation is a completely separate issue. The board has formed a special committee to handle executive compensation, taking into account comparable compensation across the region and country to ensure that our organization has a market-based philosophy. Our chairman helped institute this whole procedure from scratch in 2006, working with me and Debbie Griffith.

Beyond that, I often get phone calls from elected officials, friends, and not-for-profit executive directors with a sad story of a companion of theirs, and they ask if I can send over a couple of bus passes to help their friend through a difficult time. I almost always respond affirmatively and mail my phone caller some bus passes. But what the phone caller doesn't know is that I walk down to either our Accounting Department or our receptionist and I buy the passes with my own personal credit card. They're not my bus passes to give away, but the Authority's.

I work very hard to make sure the Authority reimburses me only for those expenses I accrue while doing company business. To take an example, our chairman, believing that I needed more balance in my life, encouraged me to join a group called the Young Presidents Organization. The group sponsors regular activities, the overwhelming majority of which relate pretty closely to professional development (seminars on public speaking, building a better management team, and so on). Sometimes, though, we do things that are more personal in nature—a round of golf, bowling, deep-sea fishing. I very carefully and in full consultation with our chairman, general counsel, and CFO have built a structure whereby I pay for the "fun" activities, even though they're built into the overall framework of YPO.

For years now, I've also written a biannual check to the Authority for $100 for no reason other than to ensure that any minuscule expenses I or my assistant April haven't handled properly are more than covered—a personal phone call I might have made to my parents while driving back from Albany at night, or a personal lunch April or I might inadvertently have expensed. Even in the writing of this book, I took care in the interest of full transparency to fully inform our board of my activities. I established policies with the greatest clarity possible, which the board adopted, and I even went so far as to solicit and receive an opinion from the New York State Ethics Commission regarding the proper way to handle this project. All the time I've spent working on this book has been my own personal time. I paid for all the expenses incurred. I even bought the laptop required to work on this project, since technically I'm supposed to use my work laptop only for company business.

I don't want to come across as some kind of holier-than-thou type, and I certainly don't want to lecture anyone. A CEO of any organization is going to do things that in retrospect he or she is not particularly proud of, and I've done my share. I am sad to acknowledge that. But if one's intentions carry any weight, I will also say that I strive to put organizational success ahead of my own. Just as getting employees to appreciate that we needed to "feed the cows before the kids get to eat" began with me redecorating my corner office, so, too, should employees see that senior executives are scrupulous about expenses and go through an annual review process like everyone else.

ACCOUNTABILITY FROM THE GROUND UP

A silo mentality used to govern operations and decisions in our organization; most people shrank from responsibility that was "out of" their "area," and they used to behave defensively when they made mistakes that were in their area, afraid Dad would give them a wupping. Now our environment is more collaborative, and people take pride in their performance. They also admit their mistakes. Our IT Department began a practice of putting up a department "report card" in hallways, meeting rooms, and elevators around our campus. Guess what? Not all the grades on the report card are A's. There are some B's, things the department publicly acknowledges need correcting. Now, the true effects of a gesture like this on an organization are immeasurable. Every employee sees these report cards multiple times a day; they're reminded that accountability matters and that they have permission to become more accountable themselves. Visitors to our campus also learn from almost the moment they step into our buildings that we're a company organized around accountability. On both conscious and sub-conscious levels, they're inspired to help us hold ourselves more accountable, too.

Individual line employees have also come on board the accountability bandwagon in a big way. Here's a heartwarming story of a guy who did a total 180 and learned to embrace his own personal accountability, above and beyond what was required for the job. In August 2008, we were about a month into our new bus cleanliness process, designed with our mid-level employee team. We had been talking about bus cleanliness a lot as an organization. I had raised the issue years earlier with Kristin Miranda, the TV reporter. I'd talked about it at employee town meetings. Although all the work selling the strategy had eased overall acceptance of the new process, some of the employees in the Service Building felt that I was attacking them personally. In fact, that wasn't true; I wasn't saying that *they* were bad at cleaning the buses, but that we organizationally were. That we lacked a good process. The right tools. Adequate training.

I had met with employees to try to get them to see the distinction, but it wasn't helping, and I was starting to hear stories that supervisors were struggling to get their reports to cooperate with the new process. As you might expect, union leadership was doing everything they could to sabotage our implementation. Around 6 P.M. one Thursday evening, I was sitting in my car, heading toward the exit to our campus. It was warm and humid out, and all I wanted to do was go home, walk out to the end of my dock, and jump in the lake for a swim. As I neared the exit, I realized I couldn't leave work just yet. I had spent so much time talking about the bus cleanliness issue that the lack of compliance was eating at me. So I turned my Jeep around and headed back to the Service Building.

I intended to park, go inside, and say hello for five or ten minutes to let people see that I was taking a personal interest in their work; then I'd go on my way. I said hello to Bob Beauchamp, a former Marine Corps Reserves drill sergeant who had been hired to implement the new process. I talked to him for a few minutes about how the guys were doing, and he confirmed that they were having problems but were going to keep trying. The newer employees were really trying, whereas some of the older employees weren't; worse yet, they didn't seem to care.

I left Bob after a few minutes and wandered around saying hello to people. I boarded a bus in Lane 3 of our three-lane bus cleaning system. This system was divided into a number of stations: At the first station, employees cleaned handrails, seats, and windows; at another, they fueled the bus, swept and hand-cleaned the outside; at the third, the bus drove through, and a machine gave the exterior and undercarriage a thorough scrubbing. An employee was driving the bus I was on, and another employee, his partner, was in the back with a broom. I greeted them with a cheery, "Hey, guys, how's it going? You guys are doing great. How's the new process working out?" Jimmy Martin, a heavyset black man, was at the wheel of the bus. He stared straight ahead. His dark navy T-shirt was soaked in sweat. He tried to busy himself with dusting the dashboard of the bus while his partner worked in the back. "How's it going?" I asked as he continued to try to ignore me.

"It's going, I guess," Jimmy said, his eyes never acknowledging me.

"Do you think the new process is making a difference?"

"Don't know, don't care."

I couldn't believe my ears. "Excuse me?"

He shrugged, looking up at me for the first time. "I have no idea."

I took a step closer. "Did you just say that you don't *care* if the buses are getting cleaner?"

"Yeah, that's what I'm saying." He stared straight at me now. Not even blinking.

"You have to be kidding me. You *have* to care if the buses are getting cleaner. That's your job."

He stopped dusting at this point. "They weren't clean before and people rode. Who cares if we get them clean now?"

Several minutes had gone by, and the bus needed to move to the next station of the cleaning process. The whole assembly line was backing up because of our now animated conversation. I couldn't believe that I had fallen into such a combative situation with an employee. For a minute, I considered firing this guy on the spot. I didn't do that, because after where our organization had been, it would have felt like a culture-of-ego thing for a CEO to do. "You *have* to care," I simply said. "It's not okay not to care."

Beauchamp had now entered the bus, saying that we needed to keep the assembly line moving. I left, shaken by my employee's honesty. When I had asked employees to be forthright and confront me, I had never imagined a moment like this.

I talked with Joe Jablonski, the director of vehicle maintenance, the next day about the interaction, and soon after I became engrossed in other matters. Yet the story wasn't over. Three years later,

I had just finished one of our employee meetings when an employee slipped through a crack in the four buses that we parked to create a town square inside one of our massive garages. "Mark," he said, "I need to talk with you."

It was Jimmy. I didn't recognize him; I hadn't seen him since our encounter.

"I was sitting at home thinking about you the other night," Jimmy said.

I raised my eyebrows. "Great," I thought, "where's this headed?"

But Jimmy continued: "I owe you an apology."

"You do?" I said. "For what?"

He looked me straight in the eye. "I was insubordinate to you. It really does matter if we clean the buses well."

A lightbulb went off. I almost snapped my fingers as I remembered Jimmy sitting in the driver's seat of the bus in Lane 3 a few summers ago.

"I was having a bad day," Jimmy said, "and I just didn't know what to say. But I've thought about that talk a lot of times, and I have to apologize. I hope you'll accept my apology. A lot of people would have fired me, and I'm just thankful that you didn't."

I shook his hand. "Jimmy," I said, "I appreciate you being such an adult and holding yourself to such a high level. That means more to me than you can imagine."

I had just spent forty-five minutes with our employees going over outstanding third-quarter results, and as I walked back to my office I realized that I felt happier about what had happened with Jimmy than about anything else.

I love stories like this, yet I find it even more impressive that our front-line employees are doing something else: taking the initiative to hold us, the leadership team, accountable in instances when we're tempted to stray. In May of 2007, Dave Masten became our new claims manager. Dave had worked in the private sector for a number of years and was an outstanding claims professional. His sense of ownership was the antithesis of his predecessor's, whose retirement we had encouraged. One day in the fall of 2008, I got a phone call from one of our state legislators. He was concerned about an accident that had happened months earlier involving one of our buses and one of his constituents. Apparently our bus had backed into his constituent's truck, causing about $1,500 in damage.

I inquired with Dave and Hal Carter, our general counsel, as to whether we knew anything about this accident. We didn't. The state has rules that require someone who thinks they have been injured by an Authority such as ours to send us a notice of claim within ninety days after the accident occurs or lose their right to make a claim against us. But the New York State Bar Association also has rules that prevent lawyers and those working with them from advising people about how to sue their client. So I called the assemblyman back and told him we were not familiar with his constituent's claim and that the rules prevented us from advising his constituent on the proper course of action. I also suggested that his constituent contact his insurance company or his own lawyer, who could advise him on what he should do. End of issue, I thought.

About seven months later, I got a phone call from one of our board members who was good friends with the assemblyman. Our board member reported that the assemblyman was screaming mad over our failure to resolve his constituent's problem. I'd completely forgotten about the issue by this point, so I checked back in with Dave Masten to understand the situation. At this point, Dave knew about the accident and had pictures, and it was clear that our bus had backed into the truck and caused the damage. Our bad. But the rules still held: We couldn't tell the truck owner how to sue us, and further, so much time had gone by since the event that the truck owner no longer could even file a claim.

Our board member said that the assemblyman was going to introduce legislation, write letters to the editor, and really embarrass us over our failure to fix this guy's truck. "I certainly hope we can figure out how to handle this and take care of this guy," our board member said. And the reality is, I felt the same way. Since we had backed into the guy's truck, it didn't feel cool to just take a bureaucratic way out. I also didn't want to belabor the issue. I'm ashamed to admit this, but my attitude at the time was: "Let's do whatever. I just want the issue to go away." I was in the midst of managing a whole host of other pressing activities, and I was now into my third conversation with our board member over a silly $1,500 accident claim.

Masten, Hal Carter, and I caught up in my office. "Look," I said to them, "isn't there some way to resolve this stupid thing?"

"We didn't make these rules," Hal replied. "The Bar Association and the State Legislature put them in place. We can't advise people how to sue us. I am ethically prohibited from doing that. And if they don't act quickly to preserve their rights, they lose those rights. The guy who's pressuring you probably voted in favor of the rules he wants us to ignore."

I couldn't believe I was still dealing with this issue, so I snapped at Hal: "So you mean to tell me we can back a bus into a guy, be clearly at fault, and there's nothing we can do to resolve this?"

Masten jumped in: "That's why he has an insurance agent. His insurance agent should know perfectly well what to do, and he knows the time frame." For a few minutes, I thought seriously about just paying the damn bill myself, out of my personal money. But as Masten made his argument again, shooting me a look of intensity and seriousness, I realized that if I just made this issue go away, I'd be letting Dave Masten down. Here I was, asking him not to behave like the woman he'd replaced, and he was succeeding. If I caved to pressure from a state assemblyman, how could I ask him not to send out Wal-Mart gift cards, like his predecessor had done?

I called the board member and told him there was nothing we could do to help. We never heard about the matter again. Now, this was a minor issue, but that's precisely the point: I do my best to hold myself accountable over the big stuff, but because we have every-body starting to think about accountability, mid-level employees know enough to call me out on the carpet on small stuff that some-how winds up on my desk. I thus have a better chance to hold my-self accountable for that, too. Our employees help me live up to my highest potential as a member of this organization, and I help them live up to theirs.

LADDERING UP TO ACCOUNTABILITY

I've described how building our capacity for accountability has transformed everyday life in our organization and improved perfor-mance. The key is to create systems that institutionalize account-ability, to have leaders adopt them, and then to sit back and be patient as a culture of accountability takes root over time. This is admittedly a hard slog, especially when it comes to regulating your own work more closely than you ever imagined. Yet it really does pay off. To highlight just how much it matters, I'd like to leave you with two accountability ladders, one capturing the old state of things at our company, and one the new:

As these ladders suggest, accountability isn't just a one-off thing; it's systemic, defining the culture of an organization on multiple levels. Allowing union workers to take time off that they haven't earned might seem like a small thing, and if that's as far as it goes, it might be. Yet if you allow that, you help to create a culture in which it also becomes not merely possible but encouraged to cheat on workers' compensation. You create a culture in which people don't care about organizational performance, and where they don't work at their best. It's the Rudy Giuliani principle: If you crack down on broken windows, you also wind up reducing armed robbery and murder rates. Likewise, by making accountability a priority, we've put a positive dynamic in place: meaningful holiday parties,

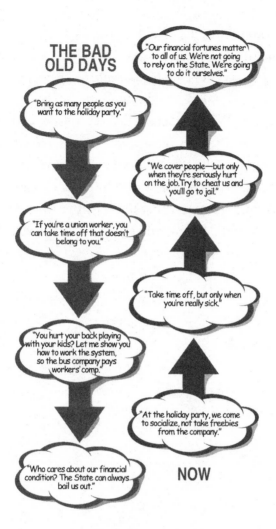

A comparative accountability ladder.

honest time-off policies, honest workers' compensation policies, all laddering up to a genuine sense throughout the organization that doing a good job matters.

A culture of accountability rests on the CEO's shoulders, yet managers also need processes in place to make accountability systemic. These processes require clear definitions of desired performance, clear goals, and a reliable mechanism to monitor how people and teams are doing. Thus we arrive at a four-letter word that is uninspiring on the surface but that in fact lies at the heart of any high-performance organization: data. We didn't become the "little bus company that could" merely because we began to serve as our own traffic cops. We succeeded because we also became data wonks fascinated with the ongoing challenge of devising better, more useful ways of observing and measuring the situation on the street. Turn the page, and you'll discover that data isn't half as boring as you think. You'll discover one of my favorite messages in this book: Estimated gas mileage doesn't cut it; no matter what kind of organization you're a part of, you can only succeed if you count what counts!

6.

ESTIMATED GAS MILEAGE DOESN'T CUT IT

Count What Counts!

I'll never forget the first customer who raised her hand to speak at our inaugural Customer Town Meeting in July 2004. She was a heavy woman with frizzy black hair, fleshy jowls, and a wild look in her eyes. She sat slumped to one side in her wheelchair, and as she spoke I saw that she was missing several of her bottom teeth. She had come for one reason: because she was angry.

"I was waiting the other day on Lake Avenue," she said in a shrill voice, "and I missed my doctor's appointment because your stupid bus was late. Then I missed my transfer downtown, and I have to fork over a copay because of that." She leveled a twisted index finger at me. "You know what I call that? Jerky service. That's right." A murmur of indignation echoed through the crowd. "What I want to know is, what are you guys gonna do about it?"

I cleared my throat, not knowing how to respond. I had no idea how often our buses were late. Sounds silly, but I hadn't expected tough questions like this. Four months into my tenure as CEO, and three months after the news conference when I had announced our Driving Excellence initiative, I still had idealistic notions about what engaging with customers might be like. I had imagined customers standing up one after the other and thanking us from the bottom of their hearts for listening to them for a change. I had pictured eyes glistening with appreciation and respect, and I had also envisioned the inspired looks on the faces of our senior managers as our customers provided strong, actionable ideas for how we could improve service and make things better. I couldn't have been more wrong.

The woman was waiting for an answer, and if I didn't do something quick, I'd lose control of the room. I shot Bruce Philpott, our director of operations, a searching look. He was sitting in the back row, next to other members of our leadership team. "Throw me a bone," I thought, "anything. Give me something substantive to say. Some objective facts about our on-time rates." Bruce gestured with his hands, shrugging his shoulders as if to say, "I don't know."

I took a deep breath. "Well," I said to the woman, "I understand you're upset. I'm really sorry you had that experience. We certainly strive to have our buses on time."

"Oh, do you?" she said, shaking her head. "You wouldn't know it. And the buses are dirty, too, in case you're interested."

I offered a meek shrug. "Well, we do our best."

The room fell into an awkward silence. We were congregated in the meeting room of a downtown public library, and on the wall was a large clock. I could feel it ticking.

I scanned the audience and moved to an amiable-looking older gentleman wearing a tie and corduroy jacket. He sat on the far right side of the room with his arm outstretched. "Please," I said, walking toward him and offering him a friendly smile. "How can I help you?"

His face retreated into a scowl. "Oh, you can help me all right. I had exactly the same problem just coming to this meeting tonight. I went out and I'm standing at my bus stop on North Street, waiting for the Route 10, and I was waiting for the five-seventeen bus, and it was fifteen minutes late."

I glanced over the gentleman's shoulder to Bruce, who again shot me a plaintive look. "Well, again, on behalf of all of us, I'm really sorry," I said. "We do our best to keep our buses on schedule."

"But I wanted to bring up something else," the customer said. "The worst part is that when I call you people, you stick me on hold forever. I'm listening to some dumb music just waiting for you to tell me when the next bus is going to come. If your buses came on time, I wouldn't have to ask the question to begin with." The customer shook his head. "No, sir, you know what, that isn't the worst part. The worst part is I've written two letters to you about this already, and the first one I never got a response, and the second it took you six weeks to send me a form letter."

My head was throbbing and my throat running dry. My mentor Bill Paxon hadn't had experiences like this. What had I done wrong? And why didn't I have anything compelling to say? I felt naked up there. I didn't know the first thing about our average hold times.

I looked over at Ann Nichols for a hand signal indicating any information she had about people being left on hold. Nothing. So I did the only thing I could think to do; I drilled deeper into the man's experience. "Look, six weeks is unacceptable," I said. "But let's handle these issues one at a time. What time of day do you sit on hold the longest?"

A woman on the other side of the room chimed in. "It's like that all the time. Doesn't matter what time you call. It's the worst ever for being on hold!"

"So there's really no specific time of day that is better or worse?"

The nice-looking man said, "You just need to hire more people. You don't have enough of them, or they're taking too many coffee breaks."

I wanted to defend our company, explain that we did have enough staff, but I had no basis for making this claim. "Okay," I said. "We'll look into it."

Then I got a bright idea. I'd ask the entire room some questions, try to at least turn this into a focus group. "How many people are usually on hold for more than five minutes when they call us?" I asked. Hands shot up all across the room. "Yikes," I thought.

I tried again. "Okay, how many of you think our buses are only on time half the time?"

Half the hands shot up. Ouch.

I had no way of knowing if they were right or wrong.

I checked the clock. Only twenty minutes had passed. About fifty more to go. What a disaster.

The evening continued like this. Tough questions followed by lame, uninformed reactions from me. All along, I kept thinking in the back of my head, "So when is anybody going to thank us for at least having the meeting?"

Nobody did.

Later, as the meeting broke up, I gathered in the back with our department heads. We walked out into the hot and muggy summer air and stood for a moment under a beautiful full moon. The meeting had lasted two hours, and we were all tired. "I don't think people are on hold that long," Ann Nichols said.

"And we're late once in a while," Bruce Philpott added, "but I don't think it's systemic."

"Okay," I said to them, "but what do we *know* versus what we think?"

Since that first Customer Town Meeting, we have gotten our act together on generating and analyzing hard data. We began not merely counting things, but counting the things that counted toward our strategic goals. For instance, as I explain in this chapter, we created a system—called the Transit Organization Performance Scorecard (TOPS), with indices in such strategic areas as Excellence in Customer Service,

> We began not merely counting things, but counting the things that counted toward our strategic goals.

Long-Term Financial Success, and Employee Success. Each of these in turn is comprised of a number of specific measurements. Our Customer Satisfaction Index, for instance, contains a large number of specific measures, including average time a customer is kept on hold, ride satisfaction, on-time performance, percentage of broken-down buses, bus cleanliness, the time it takes to respond to customer inquiries, secret shopper performance reviews, bus driver performance, and a customer survey. Our indices for each of our key strategies are in turn weighted relative to one another in keeping with our overall prioritization of our strategic goals, and it is the final combination of weighted scores that ultimately yields our overall TOPS results on a quarterly and annual basis.

With tools like TOPS at my disposal, and the measurements feeding into TOPS, I can now respond to angry customers when they speak up at our town meetings. Better yet, there are fewer angry customers these days, since with accurate information our leadership team has proved far

Data alone isn't enough—we've succeeded because we've paved a path to good information.

more able to steer us consistently toward success. A key reason so many public agencies don't work well—or at all—is that they don't put sophisticated measurement practices in place to support strategy. A school might just measure test scores and graduation rates, but these don't connect back to a specific strategy, such as "Preparing Leaders for Tomorrow." Private firms do better, but if you consider the number of companies each year that restate their earnings, you realize that they, too, still suffer from glaring measurement weaknesses. Organizations of all kinds in our country suffer from a yawning gap between their goals and the things they appraise in order to evaluate whether those goals are being met. This needs to change. Strong measurement allows firms to gain a much deeper, richer, more rigorous understanding of their business, not merely its constituent parts, but also their relative importance.

Data alone isn't enough—we've succeeded because we've paved a path to good information. Just as someone losing weight might hop on the scale every day, so strategically relevant measurements allow an agency or firm to deal with that ever-scary but essential thing—*the truth.*

CLUELESS IN THE HAYMOW

During my childhood, we would spend most of the summer putting in hay on the farm (chopping down grass, letting it dry, baling it, and storing the bales in a barn). Our mechanical hay baler counted the number of bales we would make each summer, typically five thousand. We needed all this hay to feed our fifty Holsteins all winter long, until the weather was warm enough for them to eat outside in the pastures again.

Every fall, we would begin to feed the cows twice a day on both sides of our big barn. Usually about mid-January, after the holidays, my dad, my brother, and I would climb the ladder from the barn floor up into the haymow (a loft area where the hay was stored). My brother and I would watch as Dad methodically counted the number of bales in a single layer of hay, typically a hundred. Then he would go down to the barn floor and count down the number of layers of hay. He would do this in our two haymows, determining the number of hay bales left from our original five thousand. He would calculate the number of hay bales we'd need, given the current rate of consumption and the days remaining until spring. This allowed him to decide whether he needed to buy additional hay or slow down the feeding rate and supplement hay with other kinds of food. If he didn't perform this measuring procedure, he'd have no way of knowing how much hay was left, and he could find himself out of hay and with nothing left to feed the cows.

Our company for many years didn't count the hay bales. We had become all-star athletes at not knowing how much hay we had left.

An unspoken hostility existed toward objective measurements; our leaders didn't want executive opinion overruled by inconvenient fact. What data we did have was collected for one reason: because the law said we had to. Every now and then, federal and state auditors came calling, and to satisfy them we went to the obscure office of some mid-level employee and pulled out these huge black binders filled with our data. When the auditors left, we put these binders back in the obscure office and forgot all about them.

The data in these binders included cost per hour and cost per mile, passengers per hour, cost recovery, wheelchairs boarded, and on-time performance. "Wheelchairs boarded" was a useless measure that had no bearing on how we organized our operations. It was also inaccurately calculated. We collected this statistic when bus drivers called into radio control to report that they had just boarded and secured a customer who was in a wheelchair. It was incumbent upon drivers to report a wheelchair boarded—but they didn't always, nor did the radio controller always notate the report on a piece of paper. We certainly didn't have an information system that would tell us what our failure rate was in capturing quality data in this area.

Our data about cost per hour and cost per mile, collected by our Finance Department using odometers, was hardly more useful. We don't look at these measures anymore, since we have no strategy in place that calls for reducing our cost per hour. Instead, we're concerned with revenue per mile and cost recovery. Say your cost per hour is really high. How would you know? You'd have to compare it to someone else's or watch it going up over the years. And what would you do differently if cost per hour went up 10 percent in one year? Cost per hour is a trailing indicator, whereas revenue per mile and cost recovery are real-time indicators as to the efficiency of your service. Your cost per hour might be $120, and perhaps it skyrockets to $200. But if *cost recovery* goes from 20 percent to 50 percent, who cares what the cost per hour is? It's the cost recovery that matters, at least for us, given our strategy of Long-Term Financial Success, which in turn hinges on reducing reliance on taxpayer subsidies. Calculating cost per hour was like my dad counting how much hay the cows were eating in the morning as opposed to in the afternoon. My family didn't care about that; all we cared about was how much hay per day the cows chomped through.

In contrast to the useless data we were collecting, there were so many important kinds of data our bus company should have collected but didn't. If I had been CEO back in the day, and a reporter had queried me about how we were doing, the conversation might have gone like this:

Hello, this is Judy James, Action Team Ten. Live with Mark Aesch, CEO of the RGRTA. Mark, your buses sure do drive a lot of miles. We see them all day long up and down our streets. Could you tell us how many people you pick up in each mile you drive?

Uh, sorry. Can't answer that. But we do call them "customers," Judy.

Okay, well, do you know how much money you pick up in each mile you drive?

No can do, Judy.

How about your buses? Which of them should you drive the most in order to deliver the most efficient, cost-effective product, and which should you drive the least?

Can't answer that.

Well, with high gas prices, a lot of our viewers are thinking about riding the bus to save money. They tell our Action Team Hotline that they are worried about the bus being reliable. Do you know how many times a month your buses break down?

Beats the heck out of me. Probably not that much.

Okay, okay. Forget about buses. How long does it take for you to get back to customers when they file a complaint?

Hey, would you like a donut, Judy?

Can you tell me how many times a day your buses leave a customer at a bus stop because the bus is too full?

Really, our donuts are fresh. We've got chocolate swirl.

Do customers think the buses are clean?

Well, I'm going to have a donut. Maybe two.

Come on, now. Which staff members at your call center have the highest quality interactions with customers? Surely you can answer that.

[Silence. Imagine loud chewing sounds.]

This is Judy James, live with a donut-chewing Mark Aesch at RGRTA headquarters. Back to you in the studio, Dick.

You get the idea. We knew nothing about the performance of our own company. We *thought* a lot of things, but we knew nothing. My dad would climb the ladder and walk around the haymow, literally stepping on each bale as he counted it to ensure he had his layer count perfect. By contrast, you could almost feel our white-shirted executives, feet firmly planted on the barn floor, pointing with confidence at the haymow and saying in their overly confident voices, "I *think* there's twenty-eight hundred bales of hay left. We'll be just fine!"

So often, when I speak to different groups laying out our performance-based management approach, a hand will shoot up and someone will inquire what the biggest obstacle is they're likely to face when implementing better measurement practices at their company. My response to these people is always the same: convincing their boss and their boss's boss to confront real information about the company's actual performance. In our company, because our culture centered around ego-based decisions, senior staff meetings were driven by musings, not data. Performance reviews were based on personal, subjective interactions rather than objective results. Decisions were based on "gut impulse" and "instinct."

Remember the story from Chapter One about how we selected a new model of small buses to buy for our fleet? In that case, mid-level employees had identified a desirable choice based on limited data surrounding cost factors and customer counts. They were overruled within minutes by a bigger title in a bigger office, on the grounds that their choice didn't "look like buses." If my dad had gone year after year without counting the hay bales, we would have wound up purchasing hay we needed at the last minute from time to time, and our income would have suffered. Likewise, our bus company's lack of data caused any number of problems that dragged down performance. Most obviously, we made bad decisions. If the whole culture is built around "I think," then the "I think" belonging to the person with the fanciest title wins. And so we wound up putting up expensive new bus shelters at stops where only a few customers stood waiting, leaving our most crowded stops open to the wind and rain. We ran shuttle services to amusement parks that nobody used. We refurbished a 1957 bus for the sake of . . . well, for no reason at all.

> **If the whole culture is built around "I think," then the "I think" belonging to the person with the fanciest title wins.**

More systemically, a culture of "I think" hurt us by causing serious cost control problems. For years, oversight of our Parts Department lurched back and forth between the Maintenance Department, whose job it was to put buses on the road every day, and Finance, which was more concerned with the cost of inventory. Our maintenance guys had no data system in place to manage expenses. They didn't know things like the cost of inventory sitting on their shelves, or whether we'd put three oil filters on the same bus for three consecutive days (indicating that someone was stealing oil filters), or why five mechanics were taking nine hours on a brake job that only took three hours. When maintenance controlled our Parts Department, costs ballooned out of hand, only to be excessively and capriciously controlled by Finance, which had little concern for the practical challenges of putting buses on the street. Thus our company veered from extreme to extreme, never managing to arrive at a sustainable process for maintaining our buses in the most efficient manner.

Or take bus route scheduling. From the schedule, we determine the number of bus drivers, buses, mechanics, parts, fuel, insurance, and supervisors we need. We also figure out how much we have to pay for health insurance. Yet Finance had zero participation in the scheduling process. Scheduling was driven by our Scheduling Department, which made decisions based on things like the number of buses available, the drivers we had on staff, and compliance with union rules. They paid no attention at all to data about how many customers were being picked up on the route; the cost recovery of the route; and the percentage of the bus's time that was productive (layover time as a percentage of the overall trip of a bus during the day).

To understand why the lack of data hurt us here, compare our situation to that of a major airline. American Airlines lands, taxis to the gate, lets people off, fuels the plane, loads passengers, and pulls into line to take off. If they can get that downtime from forty-five to forty-two minutes, they save a ton of money. We were paying no attention to that. As a result, the single most expensive thing that we did developed into a totally inefficient, money-draining function.

Human Resources offers a final example. Remember the overtime issue from Chapter One, the one that Pete MacNaughton helped with? The only reason our guys were able to work the system and claim excessive and unnecessary overtime pay was because our Human Resources Department was asleep at the switch when it came to measurement. We didn't measure overtime at all. All we measured was attendance. For that matter, we didn't measure workers' compensation expenses or employee injuries, other areas where we were leaching money.

Our management didn't talk about productivity or efficiency back in the day, but had they, we would have had no way to determine how productive our routes were. We also wouldn't have been able to chart improvements in performance or to identify failings. In making decisions, we would have been forced to react to pressure from elected officials, as we would have had zero empirical basis for defending our own decisions. The result would have been—and was—a low-performance, low-productivity business. We would have remained mired in a culture of "I think"—and it's impossible to win a policy debate when your argument is "I think." Saying "I think" just invites people to slap 4 percent more on top next year and keep moving along.

JEFF ROGERS'S HAYMOW

I thought about my company's neglect of the haymow as I drove home after stopping for dinner the night of our first Customer Town Meeting event. It was still early in my tenure, yet I hadn't done much better than my organization had historically done in counting the hay bales. Up to that point, I had been immersed in the culture of "I think" without even knowing it. I had solved half the problem; I was in the midst of getting our employees to think about customers. The fact that our leadership team all went to the town meeting was good.

Strolling around our campus, going to meetings and visiting with employees, I found myself walking past the cubicle of a guy named Jeff Rogers. Jeff was in his mid-twenties, fresh out of college, working in Chuck Switzer's Scheduling Department, where for years they had just scheduled the buses with their own limited interests in mind. Jeff's cubicle was where our company stored all that weak and partially meaningless data we never used. Above his desk, Jeff had a shelf about nine feet wide filled with those heavy, three-inch-wide black binders.

One Tuesday morning, I poked my head in to say hi as I was walking past. I glanced up at Jeff's shelf. "Hey, what are all those things?"

"Oh, nothing much. Just a little information about stuff."

"What kind of stuff?"

Jeff's eyes rolled; he was probably thinking, "As if anybody cares." "We have people ride the buses regularly, and I have to keep track of how many passengers are on board all the buses so we can fill out forms for the feds."

"You mean, 'customers,' right, Jeff?" I asked with a smile and a wink.

"Right, right, customers."

Walking away from this encounter, I started thinking: What if we found ways to take this unused data source and convert it to useful information? In the weeks that followed, I learned more about the data. It turned out one piece of it would help. Customer counts. In constructing our TSI, we could use customer counts to figure out how many people in the community were using a particular bus. It was like stumbling on a hidden haymow in the back filled with hay that would get us through a whole winter.

A few weeks later, we uncovered a second hidden haymow. Chris Dobson, another twenty-something employee, who served then as a budget analyst in our Finance Department, had data on cost recovery for each of the trips taken by our buses. Combining this information with customer counts, we could figure out not only which buses were being heavily used, but also which were generating more or less money from fares. This would let us compare heavily used trips with trips that relied most on taxpayer money. Equally important, this methodology gave us the microscope and scalpel necessary to identify trips used by very few people but which had a disproportionately high taxpayer subsidy. Our new, multidisciplinary scheduling team would be able to introduce a whole new kind of objectivity and rigor to our scheduling process.

Appropriating existing information and putting it to new uses was one thing, but we also had to improve the quality of that information. The information in Jeff Rogers's binders was collected through hand-reporting by staff. Entry-level employees rode every single bus on every single route at least once a year and counted the number of customers who got on and off. As a result, these figures reflected very limited data points, and they were rife with human error. In 2006, we improved on this method of data collection by introducing automatic customer counting technology. An electronic beam on the bus now tracks how many customers get on at each location and how many get off. In one fell swoop, we've eliminated human error and obtained many more data points. The reliability of our data has gone through the roof. On the other side of the equation, our automated fare box data system (activated when a driver swipes his or her employee ID) gives us better financial information, leaving us with a precise overall picture of our main business function.

We've also improved data quality regarding an issue that arose at that very first Customer Town Meeting, our on-time performance. We had technology in place to yield data in this area (it's called automatic vehicle location; in order to capture the proper data, drivers key-punch into the radio system the route they will be driving). Yet this technology had a number of shortcomings that rendered the data's overall credibility questionable. At the beginning and end of each route, the data would come back scrambled; we couldn't tell if the buses arrived on time at those points. Also, not all of the drivers would log in properly to the radio system, and so faulty data was transmitted back to the on-time monitoring system. To remedy these and other long-standing problems, we've invested millions to upgrade our technology. Going forward, drivers will no longer log into the system; as mentioned above, they'll swipe their ID, and if they don't, the bus won't start. This ensures that the proper driver has swiped into the right route, to provide us the proper information. Secondly, working with our consultants' engineering staff, we've designed a system so that all time points, including those at the end, are properly captured and analyzed. Today, we know exactly how each bus on each route on each day is performing in on-time status compared to schedule. No longer am I standing in front of a roomful of customers without hard-core data.

CSI LAS VEGAS, MIAMI . . . AND NOW ROCHESTER

To craft a way to monitor customer satisfaction, I held a series of working sessions over several months with our director of customer service, Ann Nichols, and an outside consultant. We envisioned creating one number—an index—that would give us a quantitative view of how well we were serving our customers. Yet we didn't know the methodology behind the index—the elements to plug in to arrive at the final number—nor did we know the equation we would use to work with those elements. At our first meeting, we asked ourselves: What elements would customers care most about? We came up with things like: the buses being on time, how long customers had to wait on hold at our call center, whether we missed any trips in the morning because of driver attendance problems or the buses not being repaired. All those became elements of our provisional index.

At our next meeting, we decided to enhance these elements by adding a disabled bus measurement to the mix. At yet another meeting, we added bus cleanliness as a component. At the end of our process, our index was comprised of eleven elements that together measured our customers' level of satisfaction. And since we thought it

Metrics	Unit of Measure	Actual Measure	Target Measure	Points	Weighting	Score
Average Hold Time	Minutes	49 secs	1	10	L	3
Stop Annunciation	% as observed by First Transit, Inc.	59.2%	75%	7	L	2.1
On Time	% as observed in Orbital	84.3%	90%	8	H	12
Disabled Buses	Average Number per Day	1.79	2	10	H	15
Cleanliness of Buses	% as observed by Customer Survey	53.2%	52.5%	10	M	10
Customer Inquiry Response Time	# of days Response Time	.1	.5	10	L	3
Secret Shopper Calls	Rating by Tooty, Inc.	89.88	90%	9	L	2.7
Passups	Average Number per Day	.72	2	10	H	15
Missed Trips	Average Number per Month	.34	.5	10	H	15
Operator Customer Service Skills	Customer Service Skills Rating %	80.1%	95%	7	L	2.1
Customer Satisfaction Survey	% Satisfied & Very Satisfied	65.2%	90%	5	H	7.5
Overall Score						87.4

RTS CUSTOMER SATISFACTION INDEX — QUARTER 2007-2008

RTS Customer Satisfaction Index
2nd Quarter 2007-2008

L = points x .3 = score   M = points x 1 = score   H = score x 1.5 = score

Our very first Customer Satisfaction Index.

would be cool to be like Gil Grissom on the hit CBS show, we named the finished product our Customer Satisfaction Index, or CSI.

OUR INITIAL CSI

We had the elements of our index, yet Ann and I still weren't sure if we should give these elements equal weight in calculating the final index figure. If we didn't give the elements equal weight, we needed to determine their relative importance. We wound up creating a mechanism to weight each of the eleven measurements as being of high, medium, or low importance relative to each other. We also came up with a schema to take into account our performance on each of these elements relative to specific goals. This schema involved assigning a unique 1 to 10 ranking for each of our eleven items. For example, our goal for on-time performance was to get to 90 percent. We were at 77 percent on-time currently. So we said that if we got to 90 percent, that would be worth 10 points. And if we got to 86 percent, it would be 9 points, and so forth.

This kind of thing is not normal in the public sector. We were laying out for our board, our customers, and our employees in a transparent way our goals for eleven different measurements of customer satisfaction. If we failed, we'd be standing in the middle of Main Street in our underwear. As far as customer satisfaction went, we were deep in the haymow and counting every last bale with utmost precision. Within our company, the board and our management team were really excited about the complexity of the system and the simplicity of its presentation. Everyone remembers what it was like to get 100 on a test in school. It was a simple measurement of your success. A score of 100 equaled "Great job!" Well, in a similar way, we had built a measurement system that would focus attention on eleven areas with one composite score that said it all.

We introduced this system in December 2005. Every month at our leadership team meeting, we went through the CSI numbers. Why did on-time performance improve in the winter when our drivers were dealing with snow? I can still remember the first meeting where we had a chance to analyze results from CSI in comparison with the previous quarter. Our first quarter after introduction ended on March 31, 2006. By the middle of April, Ann had tabulated all the results. As we gathered the leadership team, I was nervous; I hoped members of our team would find value in our methodology and that a vigorous discussion would ensue, but I wasn't sure this would happen.

As it turned out, my fears were unfounded. After some initial hesitation, the room was abuzz with discussion. What a huge change from our usual meetings. No longer was I doing all the talking, and no longer did everything turn on "I think"; now the data drove the discussion. It got better: In the days that followed, the team began talking about how they could help each other with areas of measurement where we had not achieved our goal in the first quarter.

David Cook, who bought our buses, was trying to figure out how to accelerate a delivery date of new vehicles to help Jerry Siconolfi improve his disabled bus ranking. Debbie Griffith was offering up her training staff to Bruce Philpott to improve bus driver customer service skills. For the first time in our organization's history, we were truly empowered as managers to affect change with knowledge and purpose. And in the future, as we pegged individual and team incentives to CSI, we would force people across our company to work together rather than in silos.

FROM CSI TO TOPS

As our Driving Excellence vision advanced and CSI results came to dominate leadership team meetings, it became clear that we'd missed a critical step. My dad had counted hay bales because he sought to ensure that we had enough hay to feed the cows until the snow cleared and the pastures reopened. He hadn't counted hay bales for sport. By contrast, we'd built this elegant index largely driven by my personal interest in providing customers with a quality experience. It wasn't connected to a broad corporate strategy. CSI was a terrific tool, but the tool had us building something that we hadn't designed and intended. We weren't acting with purpose to move our organization in a particular direction.

You see a similar disconnect between measurement and strategy all the time in politics. Individuals campaign for office, and both they and the media conduct polls identifying the issues most important to Americans: the economy, jobs, national security, and taxes. Yet once in elected office, our representatives begin to work on issues like medicinal marijuana, abortion, gay marriage, and flag-burning amendments. The media begins to cover and characterize those issues as important. They even evaluate politicians based on those issues. The strategy the American people had asked their elected representatives to follow gets lost, and when those representatives face the voters for reelection, both the media and voters themselves measure their elected officials on the minor distraction issues rather than the major strategies they were hired to address. I think it's the biggest problem we as a nation face: the total disconnect between actions taken by politicians and strategies they promised they'd follow when we elected them.

It was clear we needed to adopt customer satisfaction in some way as part of our organization's strategy; yet we hadn't taken the time to understand that key fundamental. So we went into our strategy development process with our eyes open to the prospect that we might trash our entire Customer Satisfaction Index if customer service wound up *not* being a key strategy. Of course, we wound up with three key strategies to realize our vision, including Excellence in Customer Service. It would have been nice if we had built sophisticated measurement devices for the other pillars, but we failed on that count. What we did do was build individual measurements— what we labeled as "Key Operating Measures," which would eventually become "Department Performance Indicators"—to monitor progress in those areas. Many organizations do this; nothing unique about it at all. We just had never done it before.

In the summer of 2007, it became clear that we had licked our financial crisis. We were going to have another outstanding year. As I was reporting on customer satisfaction results at a board meeting and fielding questions from a board member, I began thinking that the board, and indeed our leadership team, was focusing our energy on the limited area of customer satisfaction results, and that we weren't seeing a broader view of the company, including our financial performance. Maintain Financial Stability was our strategy at the time, and that clearly deserved the prolific attention that CSI saw. I struggled for a while to figure out how to introduce a display of financial performance in keeping with the elegant presentation of our CSI, with its weighting, scales, and point values. A few months later, we had come up with the answer: the Transit Organization Performance Scorecard (TOPS).

STRATEGIC PILLAR	COMPONENT METRIC	PLAN GOAL	Actual 1st Quarter	Actual 2nd Quarter	Actual 3rd Quarter	Actual 4th Quarter	% Variance from Plan	Earned Points	Goal Points
FPI — Long-Term Financial Success	EOY Net Income (Deficit) (000's)	$(717)							19.00
	Pension Liability Coverage	100.0%							2.00
	Cost Recovery Ratio	38.1%							5.00
	Available Unrestricted Net Assets (000's)	$17,258							5.00
	Multi-year Budget Projection (000's)	$(19,988)							9.00
	Operating Revenue Per Revenue Mile	$3.04							5.00
	TOTAL FPI SCORE								**45.00**
CSI — Excellence in Customer Service	Regional Transit Service	28.44							28.44
	Lift Line	0.31							0.31
	Batavia Bus Service	0.10							0.10
	Livingston Area Transportation Service	0.48							0.48
	Orleans Transit Service	0.10							0.10
	Seneca Transit Service	0.11							0.11
	Wayne Area Transportation Service	0.27							0.27
	Wyoming Transit Service	0.19							0.19
	TOTAL CSI SCORE								**30.00**
ESI — Employee Success	Bus Operator Customer Service Regional Transit Service	80.0%							2.66
	Lift Line	90.0%							0.06
	On Time % Lowest (20) Operators	60.0%							3.99
	On Time % Early	5.50%							3.99
	Call Center Staff Secret Shopper Regional Transit Service	90.0%							0.51
	Lift Line	90.0%							0.51
	Regionals	90.0%							0.38
	% Achievement of Incentive Opportunties	75.0%							2.90
	Total ESI Score								**15.00**
CCI — Connecting to Communities	% Growth in System Wide Ridership	-0.1%							3.00
	% of Locally Generated Revenue from Partnership Subsidies	55.9%							2.00
	Fare Stability (RTS)	$1.00							1.00
	Customers Per Revenue Mile Regional Transit Service	3.27							2.31
	Lift Line	0.12							0.68
	Batavia Bus Service	0.35							0.08
	Livingston Area Transportation Service	0.63							0.20
	Orleans Transit Service	0.31							0.11
	Seneca Transit Service	0.30							0.11
	Wayne Area Transportation Service	0.20							0.35
	Wyoming Transit Service	0.22							0.18
	Total CCI Score								**10.00**
TOPS Score									**100**

The Transit Organization Performance (TOPS) balanced scorecard.

As the graphic on the previous page suggests, TOPS incorporated four individual indexes tied directly to what by then had become our four major strategic pillars. The Financial Performance Index measured our progress related to Long-Term Financial Success. The Customer Satisfaction Index measured the level of achievement related to the strategic pillar of Excellence in Customer Service. Connecting to Communities was measured by an index of the same name, as was the Employee Success pillar.

The Financial Performance Index was worth 45 points, Customer Satisfaction Index 30 points, Connecting to Communities Index 15 points, and the Employee Success Index worth 10. The consolidated indexes then were broken down by individual measurements. For example, the Financial Performance Index contained seven different measurements weighted according to importance, including end-of-year net income, cost recovery, pension liability coverage, and the multi-year budget projection. The Connecting to Communities Index was made up of customers per mile and annual ridership. We also corrected the Customer Satisfaction Index, realizing that it was limited to just our largest subsidiary; it wasn't providing a composite view of all of our customers' experience. We broadened the index, weighting each of our subsidiaries based on the number of customers served by that subsidiary. Our largest subsidiary still had 94 percent of the point value in the newly configured CSI, since it had 94 percent of the customers, but now we had the views of all our 18 million customers factored in.

With TOPS, we'd arrived at a metric that was easy to communicate and easy to understand. And it was a metric that clearly revealed the extraordinary success we as an organization were enjoying. Tying TOPS quarterly results to our incentive compensation program had our entire workforce and our board focused on the results. It almost felt like a

It almost felt like a major corporation announcing quarterly results on Wall Street.

major corporation announcing quarterly results on Wall Street. We had rank-and-file employees asking their bosses when the TOPS results would be in. Because our bottom line impacted their bottom line. "We definitely want to know the TOPS results," our road supervisor Rick McCarthy says. "It's important to us. If the company succeeds, people are happy, and we get a piece of the pie." And there you have it: a public sector service with a private sector mind-set.

FROM SIX WEEKS TO SIX HOURS

On the hit reality TV show *Undercover Boss*, Fortune 500 CEOs go undercover in their own companies to learn the truth about what's "really going on" in their operations. The show's appeal derives from the idea of a megabucks CEO growing a beard, donning a baseball cap, and performing menial labor, such as picking up garbage or pouring Slurpees at the soda counter. It's terrific that any CEO would make time in his or her schedule to be exposed to the daily challenges the CEO's workforce experiences. Yet the show seems to suggest that this is the primary or even only way CEOs can learn about what's really happening. Big mistake. You don't need to be on the shop floor to learn the truth about a company's performance. In fact, any Fortune 500 CEO should be able to know this truth while sitting on a yacht in the Mediterranean. Quality information systems can tell any senior manager what is happening deep in the bowels of the organization better than on-the-spot observation can. The CEO's personal experience is only anecdotal information; by its very definition, it's "I think" kind of stuff. Insights rooted in "I think" might help a company sharpen the focus or quality of their measurement systems, but they can hardly serve as the basis of sound policy decisions.

Once you begin counting what counts, you start to see some amazing things. Discussions of all kinds become better. Questions our board now asks include why we exceeded plan in a particular area, why we came up short in a particular area, and what we're intending to do about our results. Today, when I conduct a Customer Town Meeting and a customer goes on and on about how all of our Lift Line (for people with disabilities) bus drivers are rude and never on time, I can take control. I explain to them that I'm sorry they had a bad experience, but the reality is that 96 percent of our customers rate the bus drivers as having excellent customer skills, and our on-time performance is nearly 90 percent. We don't have to be afraid to face customers, as many companies are, because we have key data points that tell us what the truth is. And as fun as it sounds, I don't have to stop shaving and don a baseball cap to know what's going on throughout the company.

Another extremely important benefit we've seen is a better ability to chart our organizational progress. You'll remember from this chapter's opening story that one of our customers took me to task in front of a roomful of other customers over the six weeks it allegedly took us to respond to his letter. Comments like this caused us to include a customer inquiry response time measurement into our initial CSI index. Yet we don't have this measurement in CSI anymore. During 2009, Ann Nichols and I realized that management had selected all the elements of the Customer Satisfaction Index, not our customers. This was wrong: We were the ones standing on the barn floor, pointing up at the haymow, stating how sure we were that there was enough hay to get us through the winter. Shouldn't customers themselves select the elements of CSI? So we went into the field and did some research. We discovered that we had so dramatically improved customer inquiry response time (by 2009 it was down to less than a day) that customers no longer even cared about this particular area of service. And consistent with our commitment to count what counts, since customers said it didn't matter anymore, there was no reason to continue its inclusion in our CSI. So we dropped it.

This story only had a happy ending because we worked so hard to improve our customer inquiry response time. We purchased customer relationship management software. We built an email intake system with a time-tracking device on it. We built a secret-shopper component to independently monitor the response time of our phone intake, mail intake, and email intake systems. Numbers in and of themselves don't benefit an organization to the fullest unless you take care to actually act on those numbers. Measuring what matters is a critical element, but as we'll see in the next chapter, constantly striving to discontinue dysfunctional processes and introduce innovative new ones is vital if you are to build a truly high-performance organization.

7.

PROFESSIONAL DRIVERS
OBSESSIVELY CHECK THEIR GAUGES

Foster a Culture of Analysis and Action

It was seven o'clock on a Saturday morning in May 2009. Traci Clark, one of our mid-level Human Resources employees, had just parked her car at the Rochester Institute of Technology and was striding over to a campus building where we had arranged to hold a job fair. Since our ridership was growing at a rate two and a half times the national average, we needed to expand the number of bus routes we provided to the community. That meant hiring twenty-five more entry-level drivers to run those routes. Traci and a team of our employees had organized the job fair with the goal of helping our organization meet and interview around 150 potential applicants.

Traci navigated the maze of sidewalk that snaked between RIT's tall, red brick buildings. In her early thirties, thin, with short blond hair and glasses, she clutched a big bag filled with papers and other materials for the fair. Coming around a corner, Traci stopped and stared at the entrance to the building we'd rented some two hundred feet away. A full hour before the job fair was scheduled to begin, several dozen people stood in line, waiting to get in. They were young and old, black and white. Some were dressed in three-piece suits; some looked like they had just rolled out of bed. They clustered in groups, talking and drinking coffee.

Traci made her way to the entrance, greeting people and saying good morning. "We won't be starting until eight o'clock," she said. "I'm sorry, but you'll have to wait outside for a little longer."

"Oh, don't worry about us," said one of the applicants, a young Hispanic woman with a bandanna in her hair.

"What time did you get here this morning?" Traci asked.

"Two A.M.," the Hispanic woman said.

"Wow," Traci said, shaking her head.

Inside the building, Traci unpacked her bag and set up tables in a stadium-style lecture hall where we'd administer our four-hour-long customer service examination to the applicants. Twenty minutes later, Terry Decker from our Training Department bustled in with coffee. Before coming to us, Terry had owned and managed golf courses for years. Standing high up in the back of the elevated hall, wearing his usual golf shirt and pullover with khaki pants, he shot Traci an astonished look as she bustled about at the bottom of the lecture hall. "Hey, Traci," he shouted down to her. "Are you aware that there are probably two hundred fifty people outside already?"

Traci looked up from her work. "What?"

"Yeah, the line's practically around the building. You'd think Tiger Woods was signing autographs or something."

Ten minutes later, Venetia Presley from the Communications Department came into the lobby. "It's a madhouse," she exclaimed.

"How many?" Terry asked.

"I'd say four hundred at least. Campus security just showed up."

We wound up having eight hundred people show up that day to interview for twenty-five positions that paid about $20,000 a year. Even though our city was feeling the effects of the Great Recession that began in 2007, this showing was beyond our wildest dreams. At job fairs we'd had in the past, only a few dozen people had shown up, for a couple of reasons.

First, our counterproductive hiring practices discouraged applicants. It's hard to believe, but rather than choosing from among a pool of the most qualified individuals, we used to consider people based strictly on the seniority of their application in our files. Until your application had aged long enough to work its way to the top of the pile, you didn't stand a chance. That might work fine for a bottle of wine, but not for finding the best employees. It didn't matter if you had driven a bus for twenty years in some other city, with no accidents and excellent customer service skills. Until your file reached the top, you simply had to bide your time—as long as eighteen months. And understandably, because people in our community knew how long it took to get hired by us, our applicant pool remained limited. Even worse, we didn't exactly get the cream of the crop knocking at our door.

Second, our image as an employer had been tarnished years earlier by a major scandal in which a company we had hired had embezzled nearly a million dollars without us even noticing. Week after week of ongoing media coverage showed the sheer incompetence of Authority management, which had allowed this theft to take place over a three-year period. Our organization became a laughingstock, and our leadership came across looking like fools. Established employees at the time didn't feel good about working here, much less prospective ones. It was embarrassing to be associated with us.

In 2006, Debbie Griffith had championed a total redesign of our hiring practices and our public image as an employer. Her analysis of the data had shown that something was terribly wrong. New employment applications were unacceptably low, and given our drivers' poor customer-satisfaction and stop-announcing scores, so was the quality of the applications we received. Debbie tried to fix things by turning our process on its head so that all applicants received a customer service exam and were checked for past workers' compensation claims and poor driving records. To generate a better pool of applicants, Debbie teamed up with our vice president of communications, Jacqueline Halldow, to construct a paid media campaign called "RGRTA Is a Great Place to Work." By the time of our 2009 job fair, this campaign had been airing on local radio stations for several weeks, and Jacqueline had also produced posters for display on our buses, letting customers know about our job fair.

This chapter makes a simple argument: Measuring does little good if you don't also create a broader culture in which people at all levels get excited to think about, interpret, and ultimately *act on* the information you receive. We've sustained a powerful sense of momentum in our business by striving to excel based on both the data and our strategy. This has meant paying focused attention, making the hard changes, and also knowing why we're fixing some things and not others. Sometimes we've gone back to the drawing board and fixed entire processes from scratch. More often, we've made smaller but still meaningful tweaks. We became the little bus company that could by keeping data foremost in our minds and mobilizing ourselves to perform just a little bit better each week, each quarter, each year.

"I THINK" MEETS "I KNOW"

One way to ensure that an organization actually works with the data it collects is to get people in the habit of thinking about it throughout their workday. If a data-obsessed leader is the only thing driving collection and analysis, then a focus on data will only last as long as the leader stays or remains personally invested. Get everybody in on the act, and concern with data will become an enduring part of the organization's DNA. Day in and day out, people will make data-driven decisions, big and small, that help drive strategic interests. Information will become so entrenched that people work with it naturally and even effortlessly, in ways a CEO never could have imposed or even imagined.

We do many things to bring people face-to-face with data all day long, so that they can work toward improving their performance. We've placed computer kiosks in our drivers' room; upon entering in the morning, drivers receive their daily route assignments and also learn their on-time performance from the day before and year to date, as well as their percentile rank among their colleagues. This comparative data inspires drivers to compete with one another to improve their performance. Bus drivers also can see with the click of a mouse any maintenance concerns they might have raised the day before, and they can see the mechanics' notes as to how they diagnosed the problem. This awareness that their feedback had been addressed encourages drivers to pay even more attention to their bus's proper functioning and report future problems. The result for us is fewer disabled buses, which shows up as a line item in our Customer Satisfaction Index.

More broadly, we publicize data so extensively that all employees throughout their day are reminded of results. "You can't go anywhere without seeing these posters in your face telling you how people are doing," one of our bus scheduling people told me. The posters he's talking about are our TOPS Scorecards, which we've put in dozens of locations throughout the company. As I mentioned in a previous chapter, our IT Department also posts report cards of their performance, in stairwells, on elevators, and in our lobby. Come into our offices, and you'll see many copies of our data-loaded Comprehensive Plan on people's desks. Walk onto any of our buses, and you'll find results relating to customer satisfaction, bus cleanliness, and on-time performance. Hop onto our website (www.rgrta.com), and you can download any of our scorecards for the past several years.

To further acclimate people to data, we've mobilized our wellness programs. We sponsor contests to get people to exercise more.

To participate, they carry electronic step-counters on their waist-bands that track how many miles they've walked each day. Employees report back this data and take part in team competitions to see who walks the most. Our employees also track their fruit and vegetable intake; teams with the most servings eaten over three months win gift cards to local stores. Participation in these programs has been extremely high. One young woman who works in the call center has started walking in place at her desk while taking customer phone calls. As my executive assistant April Jordan says, "I've never seen so many people around here having this much fun eating beans and asparagus." The health benefits are the primary objective here, but in the process of helping our people live healthier lives, we're also getting them in the habit of monitoring data, tracking it, and making meaningful improvements. Since for many individuals, the results have been profound ("I've reduced my blood pressure by fifteen points and lost twenty pounds!"), our people have a much deeper appreciation of the value of data, not merely in their personal lives, but in their professional lives, too.

Before, people used to avoid conflict, because the conflict was by definition personal. It was a debate of "I think," typically won by the most senior person in the room. Now the conflict is over data and information. "For years, I thought that I was only hurting myself if I didn't actually engage in a meeting," Bruce Philpott said. "But now, with our new focus on information, I've come to realize that I'm actually hurting my teammates."

Before, people used to avoid conflict, because the conflict was by definition personal.

You can see now why it was so important to create a culture of no ego in our organization. Before we can even get to a place where people are objectively debating numbers, we have to establish an environment that welcomes conflict and rigorous debate, no matter who's in the room. People

Now the conflict is over data and information.

have to feel comfortable challenging senior leadership, knowing that leaders won't let ego get in the way. Inject data into the mix, and now people have real, substantive stuff to argue about—stuff that drives the business, and the bus, forward.

WINNING THE LOTTERY . . .
WITHOUT BUYING A TICKET

In 2007, frustrated by constant budget overruns in our Parts Department, we decided to get behind the numbers and understand why. The problem surprised us: Each quarter bus drivers got to pick which bus routes they wanted to drive, but we weren't putting any time into determining which buses should be driven on which routes. Dispatchers assigned buses to routes and drivers at random, without any scientific basis for doing so. At four thirty in the morning, when our drivers' room was ablaze, it was catch as catch can.

To remedy things, we built a tool called our Bus Utilization System that applied a formula weighing each series of bus by its fuel mileage, breakdowns, labor repair costs, and the expense of parts. The algorithm told us which buses we should maximize from an economic and reliability standpoint, and which we should drive only minimally. Surprisingly, the newest buses didn't always prove the best, so we started working our middle-aged buses into the mix more. As a result, we have reduced parts expenses, overtime for mechanics, and disabled buses on the street, directly impacting customers. "We never would have dreamed of designing a measurement tool like this to deal with our parts expenses," says Joe Jablonski, director of vehicle maintenance. "We might have just kept chasing our tail trying to address the issue of parts running over budget, but this analysis allowed us to get to the root of the problem and make a deeper fix. The by-product is that our service is actually more reliable for our customers and we've reduced operating costs, too."

We're now also buying buses smarter because of our attention to data-driven process improvement. The bus we used to buy for Lift Line, our service for people with disabilities, was a heavy-duty bus that was designed for twelve years of use and cost a whopping $200,000 apiece. We had thought at the time that a twelve-year bus would give us more value over time, as opposed to a cheaper body-on-chassis bus, which lasts only three to four years. We didn't know this to be the case, since we had no data—it was just a group of people saying "I think" about the economics. In 2004, when we got ready to purchase new buses, we started looking at the data, including cost per mile, cost per hour, and bus occupancy patterns. What we found was eye-opening: These twelve-year buses could probably seat twenty people, yet our average occupancy was a tiny fraction of that. A full 90 percent of our trips had six or fewer people, but somehow 95 percent of our buses for Lift Line held ten or more.

After months of analysis, we gathered everyone on a Tuesday afternoon in the third-floor conference room. "I'd like to see if we have the right-sized equipment in our Lift Line fleet," I said to begin the meeting.

I could almost read the thought bubbles of the old-timers in the room: "Oh, here we go. Boy genius has got another one. Doesn't he know it takes buses to run a bus company?"

"What if we start to buy Ford Tauruses?" I said.

You could have heard a pin drop. Who was going to be the first to tell the CEO he was on crack?

Then the anti-change arguments began. "I think our customers won't be able to get in them," someone argued.

"Will they really be okay for our professional drivers? I think the employees will hate them," said an operations person.

As a result of our analysis of occupancy, operating costs, and capital costs, we concluded that a smaller, cheaper bus made more sense, even if we had to turn the buses over more frequently. We didn't buy Ford Tauruses, but the fact that we were even thinking about it got everyone to reexamine his or her thought process. "It was tough," David Cook, vice president of procurement, remembers. "I had been around for quite a while, and I felt uneasy and even a little embarrassed that the investment decisions we had made before weren't based on sound data—that we may have made mistakes. I know other people felt that way, too." We wound up purchasing dozens of the new, cheaper, body-on-chassis buses. Prior to the purchase, the cost recovery on our Lift Line product was an anemic 4 percent. Within a year, despite skyrocketing fuel prices, increases in employee wages, and health insurance expenses, we had driven Life Line cost recovery to an outstanding 13 percent. Customers complained initially because they liked the Cadillac ride of the great big expensive buses. But over time they became accustomed. Just like our old-timers did.

NO PAY-EY, NO BUS-EY

An organizational focus on analyzing and acting on data led us to update and enhance one of our largest business relationships—with incredible results. For almost ten years, we had been picking up about four thousand public high school students with our buses and transporting them to and from classes each day. Many of those students already rode the bus with their parents before beginning to use our service for school, so they were comfortable with it. When we began the service back in 1996, it probably made sense for us, too. Someone from the Authority had probably compared the expense of providing the service with the revenue generated from the school district, concluding that it was in the Authority's best interests to begin this relationship. Or maybe they had just said from their view on the barn floor, "I *think* we'll make enough money off this. I'm sure it will be fine."

One thing is sure: Nobody had bothered to analyze the expense-revenue equation since then. In 2004, when we had requested that

Finance evaluate the terms of contracts we had with two local colleges, I had asked them to look at the school district as well. Good thing: We were losing almost sixty cents on the dollar, for a total of about $2.4 million a year. No wonder we had huge operating deficits! We weren't just providing service that benefited the city school district; in essence, our organization was subsidizing their needs. At least we were painting the bus stop sign poles the right color.

In January of 2006, we sat down with the school superintendent, Dr. Manuel Rivera, to lay out our problem and try to come up with a better financial deal. Our team—Bob Frye, Chuck Switzer, and I—spent about two months preparing for the meeting. We had analyzed the number of students that took advantage of regular RGRTA line service to get to school in the event that they missed the dedicated school bus service we ran directly from their neighborhood. If students took a yellow bus to school, that was their one choice. If they missed it, they were not going to school that day. If students took public transportation, however, they could catch the bus that went directly from their neighborhood to their school, or they could catch the regular line service bus that went past their home every fifteen to twenty minutes, transfer downtown, and wind up at school that way.

Chuck had determined that nearly 10 percent of students we provided service for were getting to school by taking advantage of our regular route service, not the dedicated bus that ran from their neighborhood directly to school. Ten percent improved attendance was extraordinary. It meant greater revenue in the form of state aid to the school district, and it meant more students in their seats, which hopefully improved test scores. We were providing immense value that our competition couldn't provide. We just needed to get the school district to see it.

The day of our meeting with Dr. Rivera, we rode together down to the school district's headquarters. Rivera entered the room just a minute or two after we arrived, a member of his team in tow. "Dr. Rivera," I said, "we very much enjoy picking up your students. Many of them are already customers by the time they get to high school, and expanding their use of our buses while they're in high school only increases the likelihood that they will continue as customers when they become adults." I offered a warm smile. "But we simply cannot afford to continue on the path that we're on. We're hemorrhaging cash right now. In fact, I'm worried about our ability to meet payroll for the balance of this year. The relationship we have with the school district is jeopardizing our ability to provide even the most basic of services to our non-academic customers."

Dr. Rivera was astonished to learn that we were losing so much money on the deal. No one from the Authority had ever asked for anything more from the school district, so how would he have known? He was also very surprised to learn that his own fleet of buses was the most expensive to operate of any of the alternatives available to our service. We had laid out graphically the cost the district was incurring with each of the transportation providers they utilized, including their own transportation department.

The school district's director of operations, Michael Robinson, then put a concept on the table. "What if we had you pick up more of our students?"

We were stunned. I thought Bob Frye was going to be physically ill. He turned green. Didn't the school district hear anything we just said? We were losing millions of dollars picking up four thousand students. They wanted us to pick up *more*?

"Hear me out," Robinson said. "What if you picked up students at four more of our schools? But what if you could schedule your drivers and buses more efficiently? Let's say we had half the schools start at seven thirty, and half the schools start at eight thirty. Then you could bring in your drivers and have them pick up students for the early morning run, drop them at the schools with seven thirty starts, and then the same drivers on the same buses could make a second run and deposit students at the eight-thirty-start schools. Would that eat into the loss you're seeing?"

Switzer, Frye, and I looked at each other, computers, calculators, and abacuses running in the back of our minds. "We could absolutely take a look at that," I said. We went on to have some back-and-forth between the five of us about how such an analysis might be conducted.

Later, as our team walked down the hallway from the superintendent's office in silence, we didn't know what to make of what had just transpired. They hadn't rejected us. That was obviously good. They were surprised at how much we improved attendance. Good again. They were surprised to learn that we were the least expensive option. Still more good points. And they wanted to see if expanding the number of schools we provided service to would allow us to be more efficient and work toward solving our economic problem. Score it an initial victory.

But it was more than that. When we had walked into the meeting, we had thought the school district might tell us that they had enjoyed the relationship, but they didn't have an extra $2.4 million sitting around in a drawer, so see you later. If the meeting had gone that way, there would have been about sixty bus drivers, half a dozen mechanics, and a handful of administrative staff looking for work. And maybe a CEO, too. We hadn't even thought about the prospect of actually *growing* the business relationship.

We spent the next several weeks having our employees get student ridership counts, evaluating how many more buses we would need, how much the service would cost, and whether we could do the two runs in enough time to make the entire thing work. This was all hands on deck. The stakes were enormous. We resolved all of the issues except for the expense. Our costing process concluded that we were simply too expensive for it to make sense for the school district. This wasn't going to fly. We couldn't even convince ourselves, let alone anyone outside our four walls. We were both public agencies, and it needed to work for both of us.

About three weeks after the initial meeting with Dr. Rivera, the solution came to us. What if we charged the service at our fully loaded expense per hour, about $107 an hour, for the first trip in the morning, the 7:30 A.M. schools, but then only charged our out-of-pocket expense per hour, about $68 an hour, for the 8:30 A.M. schools? That way we were accounting for our full expense on the first run, but enabling the school district to enjoy the savings of the more efficiently designed service for the second run. Bingo. We could run the service at 100 percent cost recovery, the school district would have more students on public transportation and see improved attendance, and the district would save about $6 million a year. A real-life win-win. We had nailed it.

We called Dr. Rivera's office and asked through his secretary for a meeting. Dr. Rivera and his team were in a two-day budget retreat with their entire management team and couldn't see us. We pushed harder. "We'll go meet them at their retreat site. We just need fifteen minutes of their time when they're on a break. This could save the district millions of dollars a year and generate increased state aid because of improved attendance." Dr. Rivera's secretary arranged the meeting for noon the next day, at their senior staff budget retreat site.

We piled into a car and drove down to meet them. Again, Chuck Switzer, Bob Frye, and I made the presentation. Because Rivera's entire management team was present for their retreat, about half of them remained in the room during the lunch break, milling around as we spoke. Our words prompted much discussion on their side, including contributions from their legal staff and communications people. In the end, most of the heads were going up and down. They liked it. The numbers worked. They wanted to keep us in play with the schools that we currently served, and they wanted to grow the relationship. We could break even. They could save money. And more students would get to class.

About a month later, Michael Robinson, the school district's director of operations, called to say that altering school start times and expanding the business relationship with RGRTA was going to be in Dr. Rivera's budget recommendation to the school board. It would grow the size of the business deal by 55 percent. We'd go from losing $2.4 million to breaking even on a now $6 million deal. Our employees would keep their jobs. And it gave us a fighting chance at keeping the fare stable for our entire customer base. It was a huge win. Huge for us, better service for the school district, and a tremendous victory for the taxpayer. What a difference an ethic of continuous improvement can make when coupled with close concern with data.

Today the relationship with the school district has us picking up more than 11,500 students every single day—improving the attendance rate for the district—and also saving them millions of dollars a year. Whereas we once lost 60 percent on a $4 million relationship, we're now breaking even on what's become an $11.5 million relationship.

CALLING THE BUS DOCTORS—STAT!

Sometimes you can't just tweak an existing element of your business if you want to improve the numbers; you need to swallow hard and reimagine it from scratch. A great example of an internal process where we've done that is bus cleanliness. Conditions on our buses were a real sticking point for us—and I mean that literally. Sticky floors, chewing gum sticking to your shoes, used candy bar wrappers sticking to the seats. Former senior executives had sought to tackle the problem by telling our drivers, "If you've been assigned a dirty bus, you have my permission to not drive it off the property." Our buses were still disgusting; we knew that, and now we knew exactly what our customers thought, too. Our Customer Satisfaction Index scores around bus cleanliness were distressingly low. Given that bus cleanliness is a key part of the customer experience, we realized that it was well within our Excellence in Customer Service strategy to do something about it.

We assigned the project to a mid-level team and they immediately took strong ownership. I could have assigned this task to a senior team but purposefully didn't. Two reasons. The leadership folks were taxed already. Plates full. They wouldn't give this the attention it needed. The more important reason, however, was that I wanted to give a group of employees in the middle of the organization the opportunity to work as a team to solve a problem that all the senior bosses dating back for years had been unable to lick. This was a major opportunity for them to show off their game—and they knew it. They rolled up their sleeves and went to work.

Over a period of months, we wound up designing a new, best-in-class process for cleaning our buses. We rolled out our new cleaning program during our 2008–2009 fiscal year. The total cost of implementing the program came to just under a half million dollars. And the results have been worth every penny. We've nearly tripled our bus cleanliness scores. Whereas customers at town meetings used to trash us over the conditions of our buses, now all we hear, with very few exceptions, are compliments. Our buses used to be rolling embarrassments for our organization, a glaring shortcoming I'd point out to visitors and local media. Now the condition of our buses, and the interiors especially, is a point of pride, symbolizing our general organizational success. One of our longtime customers says it all: "Riding the buses is just so much more comfortable than it used to be. I no longer have to worry about my three-year-old niece picking up a piece of chewed-up gum. It's like they didn't even care before. Now you can really see the elbow grease they put in to clean these buses."

This victory was our victory as an organization. We did it as a team. And the mid-level employees that designed the solution were put front and center. I created a $500-per-quarter incentive opportunity for each of them for the first year the new process was implemented. While the "we ain't giving nothing back" union leadership wouldn't allow the employees who were actually doing the cleaning to receive these incentives, we did have a few tools at our disposal. The first quarter that our bus cleanliness results hit their new, elevated goal, we held a big celebratory dinner with them. As the guys were coming into our boardroom for the catered dinner, one of them commented on the big flat-screen TV that hung on the wall. The next week, the same one hung in their break room.

HOW −2 + 5 = 9

When thinking about an organizational focus on analysis and action, it's tempting to assume that if we improve on last year's numbers, we've had a successful year. Often, that's true. But what if our strategy has changed? Or what if we changed employees, and the new personnel hasn't been reporting the data consistent with the definition that our organization previously instituted? What if new technology has appeared on the scene that can reflect reality with much greater accuracy? Our numbers might have improved over the previous year, but that might not have led to improvement in the company's actual strategic performance. To ensure that real performance improves with the numbers, we need to take action to improve the *way* we measure, not just the processes being measured.

Is the structure of our measurement system all it can be? I've seen companies that have achieved a certain level of performance for three consecutive years, yet in the fourth year their stated goal is far less than the performance they've achieved each of the last three years. That's a failure in structure; the company will claim to have met their goal when in fact their goal was far too easy to be meaningful. In 2010, we made more than a third of our goals in our TOPS measurement system more difficult to attain for the coming year. We were pushing ourselves to perform at a higher level, since we felt that the existing goals wouldn't challenge us enough to alter and improve what we were doing. Now we might see improvement in individual measurements, but if they failed to meet the new, more stringent goals, our overall performance would appear worse. "That's how you improve performance," our chairman, John Doyle, says. "You make the hill steeper. We could easily hit last year's numbers, but for us, that's not good enough."

Another way to get better without achieving numerically superior results is to clarify how individual measurements are defined and to improve the quality of the data flowing into them. For several years, we had defined our on-time performance as being two minutes early at a particular bus stop or up to five minutes late. If the bus arrived anywhere in that seven-minute window, it was considered to be on time. As we discussed in Chapter Six, we saw some failings in the quality of our data, because the existing communications had holes or gaps in its data collection. We made a major investment to improve the technology and as a result improved the quality of our data. While trying to amp up quality, we also discovered a major problem with how we defined on-time performance. All along, we had been reporting on-time performance with a window of 2:59 early up to 5:59 late—effectively, a nine-minute window instead of the seven-minute window we'd intended. Changing the definition to be exactly two minutes early and up to five minutes late decreased our on-time performance, but it provided us with a much better understanding of the customer's actual experience standing on the street corner. As Bruce Philpott has observed, "Nobody likes having worse numbers to report, but at least we're getting it right with our definition. In the end, our customers will be better served."

A final way in which managers can improve measurements on an ongoing basis to help enhance performance is to connect measurements more closely to strategy. We've mentioned the evolution of our financial strategic pillar from its embryonic definition of "Achieve Financial Stability" to today's moniker of "Long-Term Financial Success." The Financial Performance Index is worth forty-five points in TOPS; the current year's profit-and-loss statement used to be worth twenty-two of those points, while the multi-year budget projection was worth seven points. Since the strategy is now Long-Term Financial Success, we've changed the point weighting within the index itself so that the profit-and-loss statement is worth *less* and the multi-year budget projection is worth *more*. This makes sense; given our new strategy, the value assigned to our long-term financial future should be greater.

> **We spend just as much time on the structure, definition, and connection to strategy of our measurements as we do watching and acting on the actual results.**

Overall, we pride ourselves on being so data-obsessed that we spend just as much time on the structure, definition, and connection to strategy of our measurements as we do watching and acting on the actual results. We strive not to give ourselves a pass and go for the easy but ultimately thin victories yielded by outdated and inefficient measurements.

ZERO TOLERANCE EQUALS ZERO JUDGMENT

As we've seen in this chapter and the last, a culture of high performance is ultimately a culture of truth-seeking, open debate, and no ego. With such a culture in place, management achieves increasingly greater awareness of what the company is actually doing, which in turn allows for purposeful actions that help an organization realize its goals. The point is not primarily to pursue results, but to put the best possible processes in place that will *eventually* achieve strong results. As my friend Ron Alvesteffer, CEO of Service Express in Grand Rapids, Michigan, likes to say, "If you give employees the proper tools and design them the right process, by the time you get back to your office, the results will be there, and they'll be phenomenal!"

For a leader, fostering a culture of analysis and action can be a nerve-jangling affair. We're talking about putting in place an environment where everybody is constantly raising new and higher goals, trying to build smarter and more efficient processes based on data. It's a constant experience of pushing beyond your comfort level so as to achieve organizational and personal growth. Even after years of great success, I leave work many nights feeling like we're one of the worst-run organizations in the entire country. It's the commitment to getting better that brings a feeling of underperformance, but yields industry-leading results, year after year. We always feel like we're behind the curve when in reality we're out in front of it.

You might think we are a bunch of MBA bean-counters. Not exactly. Just like we reined in Finance so that it would play a respectful role in our company's resurgence, we haven't let measurement systems and the data they produce get out of hand. As great as it is, data can't drive every decision. That's why we hire *people*—to weigh data and then use their judgment to arrive at decisions that both keep our company afloat and in touch with its soul.

If we were just following the data, we wouldn't have undertaken an initiative to put 100,000 children's books on our buses, even though that does support our new strategy of Connecting to Communities. Likewise, we wouldn't have formed a foundation that raises nearly $75,000 a year to help pay for transportation for community children to various sporting events and museums. If a private company like Miller Lite were just following the data, they would never have stopped their beer bottling process as they did during Hurricane Katrina, when they began bottling water and shipping it to New Orleans. And I seriously doubt Paul Newman was listening to data when he decided to donate a portion of profits from his consumer packaged goods business to charities. There's a reason why a person's name appears at the bottom of every employee's paycheck:

it's because people expect a human being at the top of the organization to use judgment.

People also expect leaders to show another very human trait in their decision-making: courage. Data will push many dirty secrets from the dark, neglected corners of the bus to the driver's seat, forcing your attention. As this book's next and final chapter argues, if you as a leader are not prepared to listen to the data and make *all* required decisions, even those that tear at your heartstrings, then don't implement anything you've read about in this book. You'll only be raising false expectations. And your performance will continue to suffer. You must have the courage to act.

8.

WHERE THE RUBBER MEETS THE ROAD

You're the Professional Driver, So Act Like It!

They were massed outside our building, dozens of them. Many sat in wheelchairs, although some stood. They pounded on the windows with their fists and carried signs reading, "Aesch Lies!" "We Deserve Dignity," "It's No Fare!" and "Nobody Will Ride!" In unison they chanted: "It costs too much! It costs too much! It costs too much!"

It was August 2007, and we were sitting in a board meeting in our first-floor boardroom. At issue was the introduction of our new Supplemental Service program to expand our product offering for people with disabilities. A fringe group of local activists for the disabled inside the meeting didn't like what we were doing, so they were whipping the overflow crowd outside into a frenzy. Cameras from four local TV stations roamed about, capturing the drama, as did reporters from local newspapers.

Now I know you're asking: Is RGRTA hostile to people with disabilities?

Oh, do I have a story to tell you.

The Americans with Disabilities Act mandates that we provide special service for the disabled up to three-quarters of a mile on either side of the fixed routes served by our regular, forty-foot buses. Disabled customers called in to request a pickup between one to three days prior to their travel, paying a fare of around $2. Sounds pretty good, doesn't it? It wasn't. If you wanted to travel on a Saturday, and our big buses only provided service in a certain portion of the community Monday thru Friday, then you were out of luck. If you lived beyond three-quarters of a mile from our routes, you also couldn't ride; although prior executives had made exceptions for people who lived, say, eight-tenths of a mile or even farther, we no longer did. Finally, if you wanted to go somewhere on the same day you called, you couldn't. Not everybody plans to get sick, so if you needed to get to the doctor on the same day you got sick, our service was unable to help you.

We knew these restrictions were causing hardships. For years, at our Customer Town Meetings we'd heard heartbreaking stories of disabled adults who couldn't visit family on weekends or holidays because they couldn't get a Lift Line bus and they didn't have the $120 or more that it cost for a round-trip taxi. We wanted to help people in these situations while also minimizing the burden on local taxpayers.

Coordinating with Chris Hilderbrant, director of advocacy for the Center for Disability Rights and a lead antagonist in complaining about the shortcomings of our existing service, we spent two years figuring out ways to fund expanded service. Much as we might have liked to, we couldn't just expand the service without obtaining additional money; that would have blown a hole through our budget. So after years of work, we wound up securing federal and state funds that allowed us to expand our service area by 160 percent while only charging disabled customers $6 a ride. Although this represented an increase from the approximately $2 we had previously charged, it was nothing compared to the cost of taxi service, and it also brought with it both expanded service and more convenient service (we allowed same-day bookings on a first come, first served basis, and we also offered service seven days a week). The disabled community won under this plan, and so did taxpayers: We had already increased cost recovery on the mandated service from 4 to 13 percent by buying smaller buses, but in the expanded service area we'd now fully cover our costs without passing anything on to local taxpayers.

Given that we had communicated with disability activists in crafting our new plan, we were shocked and disappointed when at the last minute our supposed partners decided to protest what they had helped us to design. Earlier in the week, I'd gotten a call from Chris Hilderbrant. "Hey, Mark," he said, "we've talked about it, and we're just not happy. The foundation of the plan is fine, but nobody can afford six dollars. We've got to do something to make the fare cheaper."

"Chris," I said, my voice starting to rise, "a month ago, when we met with you, you said this was fine. You've been to all these town meetings; these people right now are either staying at home or paying sixty bucks each way in a cab."

"Look, I don't care. We want it cheaper."

I practically bounced out of my chair. "That's ridiculous. You've been asking us to do this for two years. You didn't help us get the money; we did that. All you've done is bitch. We designed the solution. We got the funds to fix it. You said the whole program was fine, and now at the last minute, you want us to change it? You're just going to hurt the people you say you're trying to help."

Silence on the other end of the line. "Okay, here's the deal," he said, his voice hardening. "You don't find a way to lower the fare, we're turning your board meeting on Thursday into a living hell."

"Well, at least one of us is in the business of actually *helping* disabled people," I said, hanging up.

I was seething. These guys were willing to use the most craven pressure tactics to get what they wanted, thinking that like most organizations, we'd cave. But we couldn't cave, because what they wanted wasn't reasonable. Lowering the fare would have violated one of our core principles for this project, which was ensuring 100 percent cost recovery. Essentially, we faced two choices: either proceed as planned, or not do the service expansion at all. We just couldn't consider lowering the fare. It disgusted me: Here was an advocacy group allegedly acting in the best interests of its constituents, yet they were quite happy to risk scuttling a deal that even at the $6 fare would have dramatically improved the lives of those folks.

Our leadership team stood firm, and true to his word, Hilderbrant and his fellow activists made our board meeting a living hell. Yet it didn't work. Our board members, who had watched us work so hard developing this program over the past two years, were outraged by this group's tactics. The more the advocates screamed, the more they chanted, the more they waved signs and attempted to intimidate us, the straighter the spines of our board members grew. And as our leadership team stood and presented the details of our plan, our board members went so far as to congratulate our leadership, with TV cameras recording their every word. Our new plan was adopted that day by the board without a single dissenting vote. As of this writing, more than 7,500 people have taken advantage of our expanded product offering at $6 a ride. So much for "Nobody Will Ride!"

This book has focused on the challenge of taking a laggard organization and making it high-performance. It's told a story about meaningful, gradual, measurable, and sustainable change. Such change, by its very nature, requires courage. It's great for any organization to create a culture of humility, objective information, and accountability. It's vital to engage front-line employees as customer experts and to orient them obsessively around a strategy. It's also always a good idea to put money behind your strategies and to continuously

Until you as a leader are prepared to fight for your organization's long-term interests at critical moments, this entire process becomes a useless academic exercise.

improve what you do. But until you as a leader are prepared to fight for your organization's long-term interests at critical moments, this entire process becomes a useless academic exercise.

Our company thrives today because when it has really counted, we've managed to make decisions that support our core principles, even at considerable short-term cost. Courage is when you're willing to walk away from a deal that you really want, as we were in the case of Supplemental Service, because you're asked to compromise on something fundamental. If you're committed to turning around a poorly performing organization, then I urge you: Take a stand. Do the right thing. *Act* like a professional driver. Don't just talk like one. It's scary to move from a place of familiarity and safety to one of dreams and potential failure. But as we'll see in the stories below, and as we've seen throughout this book, the long-term results are well worth it.

SAD DECISIONS AND TOUGH DECISIONS

When we think of courage in business, we often reflect on individual leaders who declare they're willing to make "the tough calls." What does this really mean? I think the word "tough" is often a misnomer. In many if not most situations, leaders should take care to speak instead about their willingness to make "sad" calls. If you run an enterprise in the manner I've advocated in this book, you'll face few genuinely tough calls. Yet you'll face plenty of sad decisions that require intense determination, strength, and courage to see you through.

Making a business decision is not like choosing which house to buy or what color car to get. These decisions are rooted in subjective judgments that largely defy external guidance, whereas business decisions are mainly objective calls. By implementing sound strategy with a quality measurement system and a commitment to continuous improvement, leaders can almost always determine what the *right* call is, and unlike in football, they don't even need an instant replay. Truly tough calls—in the sense of intellectually difficult, puzzling, or bedeviling—are few and far between. And yet many decisions that we perceive to be objectively right and in line with the truth tear our guts out when we make them (as we always must). These are sad decisions. As Jim Collins says in *Good to Great*, "Confronting the brutal truth can be a very painful experience."

The distinction between sad and tough decisions might not seem so great at first glance, but it really is. Had we followed Finance's strategy in 2004 of slashing service by $1 or $2 million, with the sole intention of realizing savings, we would have faced many tough calls: Should we eliminate entire routes, stranding disabled customers? Should we lay off dozens of employees? This myopic perspective of dollars and cents left us with no objective basis for making a whole range of follow-up decisions. By contrast, the development and introduction of our Trip Scoring Index pointed us easily down the path toward our key strategic objective of Putting Buses Where People Want to Go, When They Want to Go There. The decisions we had to make as a result of TSI weren't tough at all. Yet in some instances, they were sad. We identified buses that picked up only a handful of people, and we knew that if we discontinued these routes, those customers would have no place to go for transportation. We had to cut these routes, since our TSI system had already balanced our desire to serve the community with our other desire to provide financial return to the taxpayer.

Perhaps the best example of a sad decision we've had to make as a result of TSI involved Route 95, which ran between the tiny suburban hamlet of North Chili, New York, and downtown Rochester. We had run this service for more than twenty years, but interest in it had gradually dwindled. By 2005, we were transporting a grand total of eight customers to and from their jobs every day. Now, these eight customers were extremely loyal, and we enjoyed serving them. But when we put the service profile through the prism of TSI, the results were frightening. We were spending $18,500 per year per person to provide the bus.

Let me say that again. We were spending *$18,500 per year per person to provide the bus.* For that kind of money, we could have bought each of those customers a new car and still cut our expenses by doing away with the route.

From a rational standpoint, the decision to cut Route 95 wasn't tough. It was easy. We simply couldn't defend operating such inefficient service that drained the taxpayer coffers. Yet this was a sad decision—for me especially. I had lived in North Chili earlier in my career, while working as a town employee. Day after day, I had helped these good, hardworking people with their garbage and tree removal. After an ice storm struck, I had helped get their power restored. I had chatted with my neighbors in the grocery store and the gas station. And now, as CEO of the bus company, I was the one who had to cut their bus link to downtown.

To my surprise, this sad decision turned out to be pretty darn uncomfortable for me professionally. We scheduled a public hearing to announce that we were discontinuing the service, and God bless those customers, they created a ruckus. With the media attention they garnered, you would have thought there were eight hundred people on board the bus every day instead of eight. Every TV station and newspaper in our area did multiple stories on the campaign to "save their bus." For several weeks in the winter of 2006, the closure of Route 95 was a big, big deal in our community.

One TV station went live from our park-and-ride location in North Chili to cover the story. This struck me as over-the-top; had the station gone live a few months earlier in an attempt to get more people to ride the bus, we probably wouldn't have been in this position to begin with. I was so flabbergasted that I called up the station's news director. "I don't have a problem with you doing this story," I told him, "and I think the way you covered it was fair. But let me tell you how you also could have covered it." As I went on to explain, the station could have run a "scandal" story three months earlier, saying, in essence, "Look how inefficient our public transportation systems is, spending all this money to drive a bus all the way out to North Chili." The station could have investigated the inefficient use of taxpayer dollars, and we would have given them exclusive access. The news director agreed that this also would have made a viable story. I would argue that it was the *real* story. Instead, as so often happens in our public life, citizens became distracted by the human interest spectacle of our eight disappointed customers and lost sight of some larger, more significant policy issues.

In any case, it didn't take long before the media attention around our decision to cut Route 95 led to some pretty intense political pressure. A few days after our public hearing, a county legislator called me at work. "So, Mark," this woman said, "what are you doing to my constituents? You lived here, for Pete's sake. You know we need that bus to get to work every day. People are counting on it."

I sat up in my chair. "I do know how much they need the bus. The problem is that so few people use it."

"Well, how many is enough?"

"A lot more than eight."

There was a pause on the line. "Well, you're being ridiculous. Heartless, even."

"Am I?"

"Absolutely. We have to do something for these people."

My assistant April knocked on my door, but I waved her off. I was going full throttle. "Heartless? Really?" I stood up and paced back and forth behind my desk. "Look, these are the choices we hear about all the time from elected folks such as yourself who call on organizations to be more efficient. That's what we're trying to do here. But there's a cost. It's just difficult to follow through on efficiency when it's in your *own* neighborhood."

That got her even more riled up. "You know what?" she shouted. "There's no point in even arguing with someone like you. You're just not going to budge!"

I gazed out my window and watched buses leaving our property to run their routes. It felt good knowing that these buses would soon be full, since they were serving routes that customers actually used. "It's not a question of budging," I said. "It's a question of not being able to defend $18,500 a year per person. You might be able to defend that, but I can't."

"Mark, I'm surprised at you. How long have we known each other? You'll be sorry for this. I don't know if I can deal with you anymore."

I had similar conversations with a dozen different elected officials. Town supervisors, town councilmen, county legislators, state assemblymen, state senators. It's astonishing how much energy these people put into defending the interests of eight people. If they had spent 10 percent of that energy working on the day's major issues, citizens in our area would pay a whole lot less in taxes for higher-quality public services. But this is pretty typical. Whenever you try to change something, people step up and try to prevent the change. These legislators were demanding that we provide a grossly inefficient service, yet an outside audit would have called us on the carpet for spending so much on this route, and these same elected officials would have then held news conferences condemning us for being bloated, inefficient, and deaf to taxpayer interests.

The media coverage and political pressure led up to a public meeting in March 2006 at which our board was scheduled to vote on our recommendation to discontinue Route 95. As members of the board entered for our pre-meeting lunch, I wondered what they were going to do. I knew they had been watching the media coverage, and probably a few of them had gotten calls from angry elected officials, too. I worried that they would fall prey to the usual trap of policymaking-by-media-coverage. Would they be strong enough to stand up for a policy that was clearly, objectively, right for taxpayers, the vast majority of customers, and the organization?

I worried that they would fall prey to the usual trap of policymaking-by-media-coverage.

We delved into our sandwiches and our cookies. I interrupted the usual lunchtime banter to speak. "I used to live in North Chili," I said to the board, "but I think we have to remind ourselves that the decision we face today is sad, not hard. A hard decision would be the day we have to leave here having voted to raise fares on the fifty thousand people a day who ride our buses, because we're providing inefficient service to eight people in North Chili."

One board member, a man in his mid-fifties, looked up from his sandwich. "I'm not looking forward to this vote, but this is where the rubber meets the road. We can't just *talk* about being more efficient and productive. We actually have to do it, and today is one of those moments."

I smiled, thinking that I couldn't have said it better myself.

Another board member shook his head. "Mark, I just feel so bad for those people. You see them on the news, and your heart just breaks."

Our chairman, John Doyle, stepped in and, as he always does in his quiet, understated way that demands attention, said, "I think we all feel bad for what's in front of us today. But the reason we're different than so many organizations is that we take a bigger view of the world. And while this handful of people will be angry with us, tens of thousands will thank us for providing better service without charging more."

Everyone's head nodded.

The public portion of the meeting, which took place right after lunch, wasn't without its drama. While I was at the podium formally walking the board through the resolution, a couple of customers standing in the back attempted to talk over me. "Don't cut the route. Please," they said. But in the end, our board passed the resolution unanimously, with all the local media in attendance. We didn't waver. Even though it hurt. Because we *knew* cutting Route 95 was the right thing to do. We all went home that day feeling really crappy. Over the long term, though, we'd made the right choice. The media attention died down instantly. To date, we've saved nearly a million dollars—$200,000 a year—because of that decision to inconvenience eight people. And we've funneled that money back into routes that serve tens of thousands.

A sad decision. But not a tough one.

TOUGH CALLS MEAN REAL RISK

Sad and tough calls have one huge thing in common: In many instances, they carry considerable personal risk, especially as far as your position in the organization is concerned. As leaders seeking to build high-performance organizations, we have to be willing to shoulder the risk. And that involves asking ourselves early on a threshold question: Is our main goal to keep our new job as long as possible, or is it to implement a vision? Have we taken on this new job to be a survivor or a succeeder?

Survivors and succeeders are two distinct kinds of people. Survivors are content to add 4 percent to the budget and keep things going essentially as they were last year. Their professional objective is to get the biggest title they can, with the fanciest office and coolest perks. You see lots of survivors in the public sector, and in private industry, too. Succeeders are allergic to 4 percent on top. They want to lead, transform, and challenge, and they don't care so much about the title or the perks. They're happiest spending every single day helping to make the organization better, smarter, and more prepared to handle the future, come what may for them personally.

Sadly, you don't see too many succeeders around. Which is precisely why so many organizations *don't* succeed.

Being a succeeder means being prepared to make decisions that jeopardize your personal well-being every single day. It means challenging elected officials. It **Being a succeeder means being** means taking on the news media. **prepared to make decisions that** It means standing your ground **jeopardize your personal well-** with entrenched internal bureau- **being every single day.** cracies and union thugs. It means leading your board and helping them to stiffen their spines to the coming attacks. It means knowing yourself and what you're fighting for. It means having vision, and *believing* in that vision.

Our company enjoys the results it does today because our board and senior management team are consumed with being succeeders. I, too, am consumed with being a succeeder—and I've got the battle scars to prove it. One battle that has given me many scars—and not a few gray hairs—concerned Renaissance Square, a quarter-of-a-billion-dollar construction project in downtown Rochester. I'd like to spend a little time discussing this story, because it was such a meaningful and emotionally intense struggle for me personally as well as for our organization.

SOMETIMES YOU CAN'T BEAT CITY HALL

In Rochester, it has been known to snow. And the bulk of the 50,000 people that use our public transportation system every day either have downtown Rochester as a destination, or they transfer there onto another bus to go to their ultimate destination. All winter long, they stand outside in the wind, rain, and snow, little kids in tow, coming to and from day care, at all hours of the day. As my good friend the Reverend Marlowe Washington often says, "If God had thought it through when he made Rochester, he would have made it with a transit center. But since he forgot that part, it's up to us to get it done." And on December 1, 1997, the very first meeting to build that transit center took place.

The project unfolded over the next several years. All along, I put my heart into it, spending thousands of hours pushing it forward while serving in various professional capacities. By the fall of 2003, six months or so before I became CEO of the RGRTA, our organization had finally secured the necessary local, state, and federal approvals to build our transit center. Almost at the same time, several other things happened that would affect the fortunes of this project. Our community was electing a new county executive, Maggie Brooks. She was extremely popular, and while our community had come to know her thanks to the many years she anchored local television news, she was soon going to prove herself to be a tremendous manager of a billion-dollar county government. Also, on a parallel track with the transit center, the community had decided that it was going to build a new community college campus in the heart of downtown, about a half mile from where our transit center would be built. There was real talk about building a state-of-the-art performing arts center for Broadway shows. Exciting stuff.

Soon after her election, Maggie brought together all the key players and indicated she would like to take advantage of new rules Congress had made that would allow federal transit money to fund broader community priorities. We'd be able to combine the transit center, the community college, and the performing arts center into one mega project, thus assuring sufficient funding for the last two of these. In effect, we'd be putting a portion of transit money into building the community college and the performing arts center because they would all be built as one building on the same block as the transit center. It was really innovative thinking that held the potential to remake an entire bombed-out block in the center of our city.

Maggie went and got the mayor of Rochester on board with the concept. We named the project Renaissance Square, and in January the governor announced the project in his annual State of the State message. This thing was huge. It led the news nearly every night for several weeks.

Then the problems started.

RGRTA had managed the project when it was a stand-alone transit center on Main Street, and for the first year of Renaissance Square, we also took responsibility for the entire project. However, over the next year, the staff around the county executive gradually wrested away control and built a new board consisting of the county executive, the mayor, the president of Monroe Community College, and myself. This was awkward, to say the least. County staff was managing this massive quarter-of-a-billion-dollar construction project in the heart of the city—largely with our money. And to make matters worse, county staff was doing a poor job; the project was veering substantially—disastrously—over budget.

During the summer of 2007, I had to sit down with Maggie and walk her through why we couldn't continue to advance her cornerstone project in its current form. It was an incredibly painful discussion, as I was so fond of Maggie personally, yet I needed to tell her how her staff was wrecking something she cared about. As I argued, we all had to face the fact that the project was severely over budget. We could still save it by owning up to the budget problems, becoming more fiscally responsible, and taking a new management approach, but that would require some short-term political embarrassment on all of our parts. My message didn't go over well with Maggie's staff. She was in the midst of a reelection campaign, and some of her staff wanted us to swallow our reservations and stay with the project exactly as it was. Without her knowledge, they became very aggressive with us, and me especially. At meetings and in phone calls, they'd pound the table and shout for me to "just do the right thing for Maggie."

It was a tense couple of months. I wondered if I might get fired. Fortunately, Maggie Brooks is that rare kind of leader who does the right thing first and practices politics last. Getting wind of all this, she reined in a member of her staff, and then she heeded the advice we were giving her. Right in the middle of her reelection campaign, she agreed to shift course and give the project a fiscally driven design rather than one driven by architecture. Talk about courage.

Our problems with the project didn't get any better. They got worse. Bob Duffy, recently elected as Rochester's new mayor, had fired his first shot at Renaissance Square. In a newspaper interview, he had stated that he was hearing rumors that we were thinking of dropping the project's performing arts center portion. If we did that, he wouldn't support the project. "No theater—no deal" was his quote and the newspaper headline. We weren't thinking of dropping it, but it was the first time we had seen the new mayor say anything about the project. He had essentially sat silent in meetings for nearly two years.

By June 2008, we had our feet back underneath us. We'd redesigned the project to stay on budget, and we had vetted it through a wide-ranging community participation process that had included a number of elected officials. We had even held several special briefings just for elected officials so they would know exactly what was going on with the largest project in the history of our community.

The numbers were impressive. We were going to create 3,500 jobs right when the economy was tanking. We were going to provide shelter to the 50,000 people a day who rode our buses. We were going to give the 40 percent of students who attended the community college and rode our buses an ability to move directly from their bus to a classroom without ever going outside. We were going to write a check to the deficit-laden city for $300,000 to buy a vacant parking lot that was part of the construction site. And the city would get nearly $330,000 in back taxes from the project, which we would pay as we acquired those boarded-up buildings on Main Street. This was a major win for everybody.

In June, we held a meeting of the project's board. We would have to vote whether to submit our new, fiscally responsible design to the federal government and begin the lengthy environmental approval process. Mayor Duffy was on the board, too. We had no idea how he would vote that day. He hid away with Maggie for thirty minutes before the start of the meeting. When they both surfaced, the mayor gave a rambling, twenty-minute speech restating his earlier refusal to support the project without a theater and then going on to question whether the theater would ever be viable economically. He said he fully supported the transit center and community college. Thought they were just great.

The consultants explained to him that the project was phased, with the transit center and the community college coming in the first phase and the theater in the second. If the economics couldn't work on the theater, that wouldn't prevent the first two components from being constructed. The mayor wondered aloud whether we shouldn't just build the community college on the corner of two major streets and just ditch the theater altogether right now. This, of course, after he had said that without the theater he'd pull his support for the project. Then he indicated that he understood why moving the college down the block made sense. And he questioned whether there should be more housing in downtown. And then, after all that, Mayor Duffy voted favorably with the rest of us to submit the preliminary design as it was presented to the federal government.

A huge collective sigh of relief.

Let the environmental review process, based on the design we had all just agreed to, begin.

Our next big milestone came in February 2009, when we received environmental approvals from the federal and state governments. Renaissance Square was on the road to reality. We had saved it. We had a viable plan. Maggie had been right in those dark days in the summer of 2007. We had shown the courage to stop the project in its formerly untenable form, and she had shown the courage to ignore her political staff in the midst of an election and help us recalibrate. Now it was time for the project's board to formally authorize us to create the final design.

Advancing the project thus far had cost us $17 million, and embarking on the final design phase would cost another $6 million and get us to construction drawings so that contractors could bid on the project. We held a meeting of the project's board. And everybody voted yes. No issues. No major comments. After this vote, we needed to get approval from the legislative bodies we worked with. At RGRTA, we had a bipartisan board, and I was able to secure their unanimous authorization to advance Renaissance Square. The president of the college had a bipartisan board, and he was able to secure a unanimous vote for them. And Maggie Brooks, who had a twenty-nine-member bipartisan county legislature, secured a unanimous authorization from them. This thing clearly had steam. It was the biggest public project in the history of our community. We were going to change downtown Rochester for two generations to come. We had made it out of the woods.

Whenever I reach a turning point in my life, I celebrate by buying a watch. And it has to be game-changing stuff. Like being appointed CEO. Like writing a book. Huge things.

I bought a new watch when we got our environmental approval and everyone voted yes. I was that sure. And that proud that we had succeeded.

Then the roof caved in.

Mayor Duffy announced in March 2009, after having just voted to spend $6 million on final design the month earlier, and after we had spent millions securing our environmental approvals, based on his approval of our preliminary design, that he thought we should build the transit center over at the train station. And that we should have some sort of "bus turnaround" at the location we had all agreed to. He announced that he was still for building the college where we had agreed, though in reality if we moved the transit center to the train station, we now wouldn't be able to use federal transit money to construct the college, which had been the whole idea. So without the transit center, that location was now unaffordable for the college.

And he said we should just kill the theater. Although in August 2007, just eighteen months earlier, he had said that without the theater he wouldn't support the project.

We were lost. We had no idea what he was talking about. What part of the words "final design" had the mayor missed? Just a month earlier he had voted for final design. You can't get the town to approve the construction of your new three-bedroom, two-bath house, and then as the contractor is dropping off a load of two-by-fours, decide to make it a condo instead.

On July 15, 2009, the president of the college, the county executive, and I appeared in front of city council. The mayor hadn't yet taken the necessary legislation to the council, as Maggie, the president of the college, and I had to our legislative bodies. The mayor had voted for final design on behalf of the City of Rochester, and now it was beginning to appear that he didn't have the authority to do it.

The city council, all members of one political party, said they hadn't been consulted on the project. They were right. Except for the fact that there had been at least ten public meetings and a formal public hearing on the project, which they had specifically been invited to. And not one of them had bothered to attend. And except for the three special briefings that had been held for elected officials—that not one of them had bothered to attend. And the briefing that had been held specifically for city council just nine months earlier—in their offices.

Other than that, they clearly had not been consulted.

Even had we not consulted with them, one might think that as elected representatives of the folks who would actually benefit from the project, they might have been beating down our door for more information.

The mayor announced that day that he thought we should build a smaller transit center, build the community college as proposed, and then use the extra money that was going to go into the theater to put extra decks on top of a parking garage. None of this had been studied from an environmental perspective, and it was totally inconsistent with the preliminary design the mayor had voted for the prior June. It was also inconsistent with his vote to proceed with final design that February—just five months earlier.

The meeting was a disaster. City council, after saying they knew nothing about the project, were suddenly experts on all issues related to public transportation, colleges, and construction. A week later, as the entire community watched this drama unfold, the mayor and city council emerged around 7:30 on a Tuesday night to announce they had reached a compromise. A compromise? After all this time, after all the money that had been spent, and all the votes, the City of Rochester announced they had reached a compromise . . . with themselves! The legislation that they had agreed to advance no longer involved adding more decks on the parking garage. But they had shrunk the size of the transit center, making it so small that it would have left a third of our customers—and their constituents—standing out in the snow on Main Street.

The entire thing was coming down to this: Would we allow a bunch of politicians in city hall—public servants who had clearly paid no attention to this project—make massive design changes at the last minute? Our leadership team along with so many others— Maggie included—was at wits' end. At least two-thirds of our customers would be warm, we thought. Maybe we should just accept it. Maggie didn't think so. She was so strong throughout this mess. That last month, as the impasse transfixed our community and became the lead story in the news media, Maggie and I talked fifteen times a day. She said over and over again that if it doesn't work for the transportation authority, we shouldn't go ahead with it, even though this was the most important initiative of her tenure.

Two nights later, we gathered around our first-floor boardroom table to read legislation the city council would be considering at its public hearing the next day. It didn't work for us. The transit center would have to be too small. The county executive, the president of the college, and myself held a news conference that night warning the mayor and city council that if they passed this legislation it would mean the end of the project. We gathered around the television in my office on Friday morning and watched them pass it. And as painful as it was for me personally and for us as an organization to lose Renaissance Square, we walked away.

The city was telling us we needed to build a project where a third of their constituents would stand out in the cold. And we wouldn't do it. It was perhaps the saddest decision I've ever had to make.

Amazingly enough, our local newspaper portrayed the collapse of the project on the fact that "local leaders couldn't reach agreement." I still laugh at that. We reached agreement just fine. Everyone voted for final design in February. Bob Duffy changed his mind. And then he changed it again. And then again. That's why Renaissance Square collapsed. We spent $23 million to build nothing. We also sent $24 million of funding that we had worked our asses off to get for the project back to Washington, DC, to be spent in other cities. *He* had snatched defeat from the jaws of victory.

While I am disappointed, I am also proud that we didn't let a bunch of politicians force us to build something we'd all be ashamed of. I'm especially proud of our general counsel Hal Carter and Bob Frye for standing firm in support of our larger principles and strategies. And I'm grateful to Maggie Brooks for showing me that at least some elected officials put sound policy before personal politics. We shed a lot of tears over the collapse of Renaissance Square. Yet sometimes being a succeeder means taking a stand to stop your best-laid plans from going horribly, unacceptably astray. It means that when you say "Read my lips—no new taxes," you enact a policy that achieves that. And it means that when you vote for preliminary design *and* final design, you actually build what you voted for.

IT'S ALL OF OUR BUTTS ON THE LINE

I'm not just talking about the CEO here. A high-performance organization requires that individuals at *all* levels face their fears and put themselves at risk to do what's right. That's exactly what we've seen at our company. Again and again in this book, we've described instances in which our organization has benefited from our people rising to the challenge and fighting through their fears. Employees like Caesar McFadden and Jimmy Martin helped affirm our culture of no ego when they came up to senior leaders and personally apologized for their bad behavior. The drivers who crossed the picket line to go to our Annual Recognition Dinner showed immense courage in standing up to union bullies, even looking colleagues in the eye who were pounding on their windshields. Miguel Velazquez, the head of IT at the time, put his butt on the line when he was the first member of our leadership team to come forward about his department's failures without being asked.

There are other examples, too. Our whole bus cleanliness team behaved courageously when they stood up to their union bosses and, after some resistance at first, embraced a process different from anything they'd done before. Bob Frye took a personal risk when he broke with his whole ingrained business paradigm and worked side by side with me to run our company on the basis of strategy as opposed to financial considerations. And remember Pete MacNaughton, the mid-level guy who spoke up at a key meeting and informed us of excesses in our overtime practices? That act of bravery single-handedly saved dozens of jobs and made our organization more efficient.

I'm proud of all these individuals. But I'm especially proud of the courage our leadership team has shown. You'll remember that when I became CEO, we didn't have a cohesive team running things at the top. We had to build one, meshing our personalities into one group where people felt comfortable sharing their opinions. To my delight, our leadership team has collectively risen to meet the hardest challenges. We've shown that we're a team of succeeders, not survivors. And I'd like to share with you one last story that illustrates this.

RGRTA VS. THE UNITED STATES GOVERNMENT

In January 2007, after we had renegotiated our innovative public-public partnership with the City of Rochester School District, our federal regulatory agency, the Federal Transit Administration, stepped in and ordered us to stop. They didn't seem to mind when we were losing our shirts on the service. But when we fixed the relationship so it actually made sense economically, and when we grew the number of students to whom we provided service—well, that's when the federal government stepped in.

We asked them to reconsider, pointing out that there were two problems with their lack of logic. One, nearly every city in the United States of America provided service that was similar to what we provided, except that they lost money on it, just as we had for years. Why should we be penalized for coming up with a better solution? Second, the feds' order to stop was founded in the notion that we were now providing *too much service*, that the scope of the service was somehow the problem. We argued that if we could pick up 4,000 students a day for more than twelve years and it was fine then, surely it was fine to pick up 11,500 students a day now. They disagreed and ordered us again in August 2007 to stop.

I still remember exactly where I was when the federal administrator I was speaking with said she was reaffirming the agency's initial decision. It was late on a Friday afternoon. April forwarded the administrator's call to my cell phone. School was going to open in about a month and the federal government was ordering us to not pick up schoolchildren.

Hal Carter had joined our team by then. He had been our lead attorney at the outside law firm the Authority had used for decades. Hal was so incredibly capable, so passionate, and so prodigious in his work output that bringing him inside our four walls strengthened us immeasurably. A tall guy, balding, Hal worked very hard at keeping himself in shape. He had a variety of interests, and somehow he managed to balance them all and still excel at just about everything he touched. He was particularly good at his job.

The two of us talked the issue over for a day or two. This was a big deal. We then talked it through with our chairman, John Doyle. The path was clear. We were going to sue our federal regulatory agency in federal court. An even bigger deal. And risky. Here was a regulatory body telling us we couldn't do something. These were the same people who controlled tens of millions of dollars in aid coming to us every year. If we pissed them off, we faced the real risk that all of our money to buy buses would be shut off. Even if we were to win this case, every audit in the future, for years to come, might be done in a minute, nitpicky way. Our regulators might write scathing audits claiming that we had stapled pages together on the left-hand side as opposed to the right-hand side. We could win the case and still lose big as an organization.

But would we win? The likelihood of a federal court overturning a federal regulatory agency is very low. We thought we had a strong argument, but federal judges typically give these regulatory bodies pretty wide latitude. Our case was by no means a slam dunk. Yet we were determined to do the right thing. We had arrived at an arrangement with the city schools that was a win-win for everyone, including our organization. We couldn't let that go without a fight.

We filed suit and the federal judge, David Larimar, stepped in immediately. He wasn't about to have kids without a way to get to school in a week. He issued a stay and ordered the parties to try to work this out. We then exchanged letters with our regulators asking for clarification of their decision. We said that there was a reason there were regulations governing how to provide this kind of service, and while it was conceivable that we were doing it the wrong way, despite their having approved it for the past twelve years, there clearly was a right way to provide the service. Otherwise there wouldn't be regulations. The federal government doesn't have regulations on how to smoke crack on a street corner, because you're not supposed to do that. They do have regulations on how public transportation systems can pick up schoolchildren because you are allowed to do that.

The FTA agreed to meet with us in New York City in October. They brought in their Mr. Big attorney from Washington, DC. It was clear very quickly that they didn't care what we had to say. We met in the FTA offices a few hundred yards from Ground Zero, on the fourth floor of a historic building. Our team entered a square conference room with a rectangular table with room for maybe a dozen people and chairs along the walls for another dozen or so, with windows open to a courtyard. Representing our side were Hal, Michael Robinson (the school district's director of operations), Chuck Switzer, Ryan Gallivan (a member of Chuck's Scheduling Department), and me. On the FTA's side were the FTA regional administrator and the deputy administrator, their Mr. Big attorney, and their regional counsel.

We began by laying out for them a different approach as to how we intended to provide service so that schoolkids could ride our buses. And we laid out why we believed our plan complied with federal regulations. "There clearly is a right way to pick up school students," I remarked. "The regulations provide for it. Now, it's conceivable that we're not doing it the right way. We think we are; you say we're not. But there is a right way. So if we're doing it wrong, as you keep saying, help us design the right way."

Mr Big (he was actually short, with curly hair, balding, early thirties) kept coming back to the following point: "The role of the FTA is not to tell you how to do something. It's to ensure compliance."

"Well," someone on our side said, "even the IRS helps you fill out your taxes."

Mr. Big sat back in his chair and yawned. "It looks like you've gotten closer with this new approach that you're talking about, but we don't think it's going to fly."

Hal shook his head. "We're clearly missing something here. We've picked up four thousand students for years, losing our shirt on it, and you've always said it was fine. The only thing we've changed is we're picking up more students and we're not losing money on it. And there's nothing in the regulations that speaks to volume or profitability."

People on their side were looking at the clock. It was clear that they'd had enough. Someone, I don't remember who, ended things by saying: "Look, it was good that the judge suggested we convene to talk through this, but we haven't seen anything that would change our position. We'll just have to litigate this, I'm afraid."

The FTA had decided that our business approach to actually covering our costs in providing the service, and the fact that we picked up so many students, were somehow in violation of their regulations. Some weeks later, they issued another letter describing our approach as impermissible. These regulators were assuming that we'd be like most transit systems and back down, deferring to their decision. They probably felt there was very little chance that we would actually pursue this in court. We had a discussion internally about whether to go forward. The risks were great, but we all agreed: We would do the right thing here. We would sue.

It was a decision of which I'll always be proud. A decision that our leadership team made together.

OUT THERE ON THE PARKING ISLAND

Just before Christmas, we made our oral arguments in the FTA case. The courtroom was tense. I really felt pressured. There was a lot at stake here. Jobs. Kids getting to school. Our business approach. The cost to the school district and taxpayers if they couldn't take advantage of the partnership we had designed. Also, this case had big-time national implications. The national public transportation industry was watching. Urban school districts were watching. Private school bus carriers were paying attention, smelling a potential business opportunity in the event that our arrangement was ruled illegal. Public employee unions also were watching; some on the public transportation side feared they were going to lose work, while some on the school bus side anticipated that they might gain work.

After the oral argument, we had to wait several weeks for a decision. It was excruciating. On January 24, 2008, I was standing out in the cold on the concrete island in front of our security shack, waiting for New York State Assemblyman David Gantt to arrive. He and I were about to hold a news conference unveiling the 1957 bus that we had refurbished for use as a public education tool. Remember that bus? We did eventually come up with a purpose for it. We planned to use it as part of a school program to remember an ugly time in American history when not all public transportation customers were treated the same. We had invited Assemblyman Gantt over because he had gotten an earmark of state dollars for us to cover the refurbishment.

I was standing on the island, casually talking with one of our superstar bus drivers, Jim Peasley, when Hal Carter, Chuck Switzer, and Steve Hendershott came racing over and pulled me aside. They had been over in the main garage waiting with a bunch of our employees and the assembled news media for the event to begin. Excitement radiated from Hal's eyes. "The decision is in," he said. His breath froze as he spoke in the cold winter air. "They're still reading it over at the law firm. But it looks like we won. On every issue!"

Chuck and Steve were literally jumping up and down. We all hugged. I can only imagine what it looked like to people watching from windows above in our Administration Building. Four executives of the company, standing out in the freezing cold, wrapped in winter coats, embracing like crazy people.

We exchanged some strategy ideas. How should we tell the news media? What would we say at this event right now? How would we inform the school district? How would we gather our employees? And then my three colleagues were gone. And I was alone. Standing in the cold by myself. On an island. With all the weight of the world lifted off my shoulders.

I'd never known what it felt like to have a weight lifted off you, but I learned that cold January morning. We had won because we were right. We'd taken on the federal government. And we'd won!

We notified our board, who were as excited as we were. And after the news media had left the property, we met with all of our employees and had a wild celebration. Our victory was their victory. We had won as a family. Then we held a news conference with the superintendent of schools. Dr. Rivera had recently left. Jean-Claude Brizard and I announced to the community what this victory meant for local taxpayers, how it would allow more students to get to class, and how it demonstrated that the rule of law *does* matter.

Because we stood tough, our service to the Rochester City School District and its students is today stronger than ever, and the benefit to the taxpayers is greater than ever. Even better, the retribution we'd anticipated from the FTA turned out to be a non-issue. Despite our differences on this issue, members of the FTA have proved to be phenomenal professionals. Once this issue regarding the school district was closed, our relationship with the regional FTA office improved dramatically. Through the deepest days of the Renaissance Square issues, the FTA was outstanding in evaluating information and making quick decisions. On that dark day when city council passed legislation that killed the project, the staff in the FTA office was every bit as devastated as those of us on the ground. Overall, we've seen no negative consequences because of our decision to go to court. Just the opposite: The FTA has been fantastic.

This episode, and the book as a whole, just goes to show that strong leadership *can* make a difference and help a struggling organization become the little bus company that could. If we can do it here in snowy Rochester, New York, then your dysfunctional organizations can, too. Take a stand. Stay strong. Fight the good fight. Victory, when it comes, is wonderful to experience.

Epilogue

THE ROAD TO
REVOLUTIONARY RESULTS

This book has laid out a program for turning laggard enterprises into industry-leading ones. We've talked about culture, strategy, creating systems of accountability, putting measurement systems in place linked to strategy, and making improvements based on the data generated—all building up to a hybrid, public-private approach to running an organization. We've also affirmed something very basic: The importance of good old-fashioned leadership. To turn our organizations around and drive excellence, we really do need people in place who are prepared to make painful, sad, risky decisions when it counts. We need people ready to fight for what is right. We need succeeders, not survivors.

Like many Americans, I've become concerned about the apparent decay in our country, its institutions, and its organizations. The media offers a never-ending flood of stories about corporate malfeasance, elected officials who sacrifice the public good for personal gain, proud American icons like General Motors on the verge of bankruptcy, and public agencies that charge more and do less. How are we going to compete with emerging twenty-first-century powerhouses like China, India, and Brazil? And how are we going to put our country on a path to fiscal health? How are going to sustain the prosperity and growth to which we've become accustomed?

These problems have been with us for a while now—so long, in fact, that it's easy to wonder whether we'll ever find viable solutions. We've heard optimistic talk from politicians on both sides of the aisle, yet too often they deliver deficits, tax hikes, double digit spending increases, and underperforming stock prices. The story of the RGTA offers reason for hope. It affirms that there *is* a way out of our economic malaise, and that the solution doesn't come from on high in the form of a massive new government program or bailout, nor does it require adherence to a particular political ideology, or increased spending or higher taxes. If leaders in business and government can just discipline themselves and apply some simple, down-on-the-farm principles of sound management, then the solution will begin to bubble up from below, as organizations big and small reinvent themselves to become far more efficient and productive than anyone thought possible.

People I speak to are shocked that the RGRTA could achieve the results that we have in today's environment, largely because almost nobody else is doing it. But think about it: If a mid-size bus company in Rochester, NY, on the verge of bankruptcy can turn itself around in a couple of years against the pull of entrenched interests, then larger, merely underperforming agencies and companies could do even more. And our economy as a whole would look radically different than it now does.

What if the school districts in Dallas, Detroit, and Dubuque could improve efficiency, reduce property taxes, and increase graduation rates and standardized test scores?

What if the airlines ran on time, didn't charge you for luggage, and focused their attention on *your* happiness?

What if the federal government could increase revenue from tax cheats rather than raising taxes on the rest of us, decrease regulations on businesses that unnecessarily boost costs for end consumers, and improve the efficiency of agencies like Amtrak or the Postal Service?

What if we got organizations of all kinds to focus on *why* they exist—rather than on getting 4 percent larger each year?

You might object that meaningful change is easier said than done, and of course, you're right. It will require strong will on the part of leaders to depart from business as usual and aim for something better. We at the RGRTA didn't *have* to reform ourselves. We could have just shown up doing business as usual, relying on federal and state governments to bail us out. They would have given us the $27.7 million to cover our projected losses without demanding any reforms on our part. That's standard practice in public finance. Instead, we not only fixed what ailed us, but have built more than $30 million in surpluses while providing superior customer service. Imagine if government gave all that money back to taxpayers. And imagine if there were ten other transit organizations like ours that did the same thing. Imagine if school districts, and hospitals, and General Motors, and CitiBank all did that. Now you're talking real change!

Organizations don't exist in a vacuum. For change to take place on a national scale, we need to toss on the trash heap those structures and systems that perpetuate the status quo. One place to begin is the process that exists for allocating public monies. A problem we initially faced when I became CEO was that bureaucrats weren't evenly distributing precious state dollars to all transportation systems. We were getting screwed. We lobbied, and partially on the basis of the reforms we were making, we achieved equity in state aid. But then something incredible happened. In 2007, then Governor Elliot Spitzer proposed *cutting* our state aid allocation because of how well we had performed. Yes, you heard that correctly. Because we had a strong bottom line, had built a strong foundation, and had used our state increase of $3 million the prior year not for general operations, but for expanded Supplemental Service for people with disabilities, the governor decided we didn't "need" our existing level of funding. And so he recommended our state aid be cut and given in increased aid to other underperforming transit systems.

We didn't just object to Spitzer's decision, but to its underlying philosophy. Government bureaucrats in both parties have enjoyed an ability to arbitrarily deliver bailouts to communities, and to make this practice look good, they label it a "needs based" distribution model. "Needs based" is a fancy way of saying if you need a new party dress, a higher level of government will give you one. State government almost encouraged organizations like ours to be unproductive and inefficient; they would give you more money because you "needed" it. This might sound astonishing, but it's absolutely true. If an organization in one part of the state threatened a fare increase due to money troubles, state bureaucrats would throw money at it. If another organization had a strong bottom line, bureaucrats would take money from them and give it to the struggling organization. Of course, the strong organization would wind up weak the following year and as a result would "need" more. This circular firing squad mentality certainly kept the bureaucrats busy, which I suspect was the main idea.

In countering Governor Spitzer's proposal, we argued that government should distribute aid according to an objective formula, providing us with the same level of funding that sister public transportation agencies enjoyed. We wanted bureaucrats to evaluate us for aid on a *performance-based* criteria, rather than a "needs based" one. As we saw it, there should be a baseline of aid distributed equitably according to the number of taxpayers using the service, and on top of that government should provide an incentive that would reward higher-performing systems for providing a more efficient and productive level of service. Because of our new commitment to driving productivity, we believed we would stack up well against others in a competitive, performance-based environment, driving additional revenue to our bottom line. But that wasn't our main motivation. If some other organization excelled in a particular area, then we'd have a chance to go learn from them. We also hoped to build a competitive spirit among our colleagues at other transit systems, leading to an across-the-board end to mediocrity. All of us could achieve financial stability by working toward high performance under a new, more level, competitive playing field.

I'm happy to say that we won the initial battle. In the spring of 2008, we received a $3.4 million increase in state aid from the legislature over what Governor Spitzer had proposed. In true dollars, this represented just a $410,000 increase over the previous year, but the message it sent the state bureaucracy and the governor was powerful. Performance matters. State aid should not be handed out to those organizations that simply need it, but rather to those that have *earned* it.

And in 2009, when Governor David Paterson cut our state aid we actually sent him a thank you letter. Because his reductions were not targeted at organizations like ours that were strong. His cuts were equitable and across the board. Every organization was reduced. When times are tough, everyone learns to do more with less. The days of stealing from the strong and bailing out the underperformers had passed.

Today, we're working to make performance-based state aid the law of the land. Legislation has been introduced to require that 70 percent of public transportation dollars be distributed in a fair and equitable fashion; 25 percent distributed according to performance metrics, whereby the highest performer gets more in state aid; and only 5 percent left to the discretion of state bureaucrats to bail out bus companies in trouble. The "needs based" model we set out with now has a stake driven through its heart, and transportation customers and taxpayers alike are beginning to benefit.

Succeeding in New York is great, but we need *all* public transportation systems in America focused on high performance. And all city governments. And all electric companies, banks, and construction companies. And the US military. The list goes on and on.

America can put itself on the path to renewal, but our days of distraction need to end. We need to stop chasing the next "shiny thing" that news media, elected officials, and senior business executives shake in front of us so that we won't notice their hand in our pocket and zero points on the scoreboard. We need courageous leadership and discipline to eradicate the plague of massive overspending at the federal and state levels. We need a national political culture in which no-ego, responsibility, and data-based decision-making reign. Most of all, we need the courage to dream—and act—big.

The choice is ours. If we continue on our present course, America's institutions and organizations might survive a while longer. But if we apply sound management on the organizational and societal levels—a set of principles that any small businessperson or family farmer knows too well—then we can follow the trail blazed by the little bus company that could, and *succeed*.

RULES OF THE ROAD

1.

NOBODY KNOWS THE DRIVER'S NAME
Create a Culture of No Ego

- When your goal is to radically transform a company and improve its performance, changing the culture is every bit as important as changing the balance sheet.
- Feed the cows first—help employees realize that their needs don't come before their work.
- *Be* in charge. Don't just do things that make it *seem* like you're in charge.
- Make it okay for subordinates to challenge you.
- Open yourself up to contributions from everyone, even mid- or lower-level employees who rarely are consulted. Help the people who do the work identify the problem and design the solution.
- People are watching; even small, seemingly insignificant gestures on the part of management count for a lot.
- Culture doesn't change overnight. Be patient and keep slogging away. It will change.

- When trying to build a culture of no ego, make sure to celebrate. Help everyone realize that success is everyone's win.

2.

THE MARKETPLACE IS BIGGER THAN YOUR BUS
Listening Means More Than Just to Customers

- Often employees in the trenches know what customers want even more than the customers themselves do.
- Even uncooperative or bitter employees can eventually contribute. Don't write them off!
- In every company, you'll find brave line employees who will buck the pressure from union thugs. Help them be brave.
- Build into the company's structure the process of listening to employees. If employees are consulted on a routine basis, they'll feel more convinced that management takes them seriously.
- As the first order of business in employee feedback meetings and work sessions, make sure you follow up on the implementation of takeaways from the last session. That way, employees can see that their contributions are making a difference.
- Don't content yourself with employee contributions alone. Many employee ideas about customers are just kernels. They require research and analysis from the actual marketplace.

3.

THE BUS IS LEAVING, SO GET EVERYBODY ON BOARD!
Sell Your Organization on the New Strategic Direction

- Leave the Sunday afternoon drive to folks when they retire. When you're working, drive someplace—and tell people where you're going.

- Make sure you understand the strategic relevance of each tactic. Know why you are putting in hay, rather than just hooking up the baler.
- Pose and answer the question of what you require in order to achieve your mission and vision. Don't just continue doing what you do today for its own sake.
- When you've picked the path, sell *all* the constituencies: customers, employees, management, media, elected officials, shareholders, and the board.
- Sometimes the best way to help employees understand where you're going is to just "hang out." Take advantage of teaching opportunities as they present themselves.
- Walking the path will scare folks. Be available. Listen. Test what you hear. Make adjustments as necessary; it's a new path and there will always be potholes.
- Again, be patient. Employees will not all jump on board with a strategy overnight. Give your strategies the time they need to sink in.

4.

CHART YOUR ROUTE, *THEN* FILL THE TANK
Spend Money Purposely to Support Your Strategy

- A financially managed company isn't the same as a financially successful one.
- Be sure to lead. Finance will fill a vacuum of control if there is no vision coming from the top.
- Be on guard lest Finance try to make decisions in areas beyond its purview. Just because there's money involved doesn't mean Finance should be in charge.
- Look hard at all your processes throughout the company. Are there areas where Finance is in charge but shouldn't be?

- Make budgeting a collaborative process; share it with leadership and line employees before it's done. Give them the chance to appeal.
- Connecting spending to strategy means effecting change. Expect attacks and blowback.
- Most financial executives seek financial success rather than personal power. Getting them to swim in their own lane will make them personally happier even as it makes the organization richer.

5.

TO AVOID GETTING A TICKET,
WATCH YOUR OWN SPEEDOMETER
Embrace Accountability in All That You Do

- Help employees feel safe enough to challenge you. When they feel safe enough, they'll hold themselves accountable and present bad news without being "caught."
- Connect incentive compensation to strategy. Make those opportunities both broad (financial results) and specific to daily work activities (e.g., on-hold times).
- Picking up nails for a penny means it has to be the entire nail. Close doesn't cut it.
- Put enough money into incentives to get people's attention. Pay some on a quarterly basis; people need to see that immediate improvement produces immediate compensation.
- Be precise with definitions. Make sure everyone knows what an A is.
- Identify in writing how a successful year will be defined before the year begins.
- Compare your performance to that of others and do it systemically. You only know you're great if you're better than somebody else—and if you stay better.

- Today employees might not *care* if the bus is cleaner, they might just clean it. Tomorrow, they might actually care.
- Crack down on the loopholes and giveaways. Make it clear that lapses in accountability won't be tolerated.

6.

ESTIMATED GAS MILEAGE DOESN'T CUT IT
Count What Counts!

- Appreciate the connections between a culture of no ego and data. Egotistical behavior will persist if every conversation begins with "I think." In that case, the opinion possessed by the person with the biggest title will always win, rather than the opinion that reflects the most knowledge. Data matters.
- The less information you have, the more open you are to attacks and criticism from employees, customers, taxpayers, shareholders, elected officials, media, and board members.
- Count only those things that further your strategies. Measuring things that are merely interesting distracts everyone.
- An on-time bus is more important than a clean one. Weight your measurements to focus attention on what really matters.
- A lot of people work very hard to avoid knowing how their organization is performing. Don't be one of them.
- *Undercover Boss* is a cool reality show, but don't confuse individual observation with quality information systems. Personal observation should *sharpen* your measurements, not replace them.
- When measuring customer satisfaction, let the customers decide what gets measured and what should be weighted the heaviest.
- Don't just pick off-the-shelf measurement methods and tools. Get creative. Come up with measurements that really do match your business processes.

225

- If you have measurement systems in place, great. Now make sure you change them to match changes in your business, your markets, and your performance.

7.

PROFESSIONAL DRIVERS OBSESSIVELY CHECK THEIR GAUGES
Foster a Culture of Excellence

- Open yourself to change. Dramatic and sustained improvement won't come from doing things the same old way.
- Hiring more people to scrub buses will not get them cleaner. Throwing money at underperformance will not drive results. System redesign will.
- Post the results. The good ones, the bad ones, the ones in the middle. Let everybody see where you're hitting your numbers and where you're failing.
- Don't obsess about the broader results, but rather about the processes that comprise the foundation of your business. With the foundation constructed the right way, fantastic results will fall right out of the sky.
- The buggy whip factory learned how to make headlights for cars. Evolution of systems and process needs to be constant.
- Continually look for the most productive new way to perform routine tasks. The cows need hay; they don't know if it's wrapped in labor-intensive wire bales or not.
- Learn from others. You don't have to come up with every good idea—especially when someone is better than you are today.
- They hire people for a reason. Use some judgment! Don't rely on the data to do everything.

8.

WHERE THE RUBBER MEETS THE ROAD

You're the Professional Driver, So Act Like It!

- High performance requires high personal risk. If you're going to be a leader, be prepared to swallow hard and jump.
- There is a big difference between sad decisions and tough ones. Most decisions are sad. Work to know the difference.
- The world has a lot of survivors. Be a succeeder instead.
- Sometimes taking a courageous stand happens over years. Stay strong. Keep on the path.
- When line employees see the bosses picking success over survival, sometimes they'll cross a picket line. Be aware of the power of example.
- You can't always beat city hall, but don't let that discourage you from taking risks.
- Courage isn't just about the CEO. Entire organizations and teams within organizations need to learn how to behave courageously.

THE RGRTA TURNAROUND

Key Dates

April 2004	Mark Aesch is appointed CEO of RGRTA. Organization faces a multimillion-dollar operating deficit threatening employee layoffs, fare hikes, and massive service reductions.
May 2004	Major customer service initiative called Driving Excellence is announced.
July 2004	Special retreat for leadership team held to create competency for open debates.
December 2004	John Doyle is elected chairman of the board.
July 2005	Establishment of our new annual planning process that ensured financial goals were supporting a vision.
September 2005	Results of new Trip Scoring Index are introduced, balancing customer demand with taxpayer subsidies. "Empty Buses Are Not Good" radio campaign is on the air.
December 2005	We institute our first composite measurement tool—the Customer Satisfaction Index.

February 2006	Development of our first Strategic Plan with three key strategies: Achieve Financial Stability, Excellence in Customer Service, and Putting Buses Where People Want to Go When They Want to Go There.
March 2006	New fare structure with one price for every customer all the time is introduced.
March 2006	First Comprehensive Plan is unanimously adopted by the board.
May 2006	We negotiate an innovative business deal with the Rochester City School District that saves them millions, improves school attendance, and corrects an upside-down business deal for us.
March 2007	We finish fiscal year with an $8.1 million surplus after losses of $4.3 million and $5.1 million the years prior.
August 2007	We implement a massive expansion of service for people with disabilities and face protests for doing it.
January 2008	We win a landmark lawsuit against the Federal Transit Administration allowing our deal with the Rochester City School District to continue.
April 2008	We build a comprehensive balanced scorecard called TOPS that measures quarterly performance on each of our key strategies.
August 2008	Mid-level employees design and implement a total overhaul of our bus cleanliness process, dramatically improving results.
September 2008	We reduce fares for our customers—ridership skyrockets.
May 2009	With the reform of our employee recruitment process, we run an aggressive advertising campaign attracting hundreds of applicants.
June 2009	One of our employee unions agrees to a pay for performance incentive compensation program.

July 2009   Renaissance Square, a quarter-billion-dollar construction project in the heart of downtown Rochester, is killed by the city after the mayor had just voted for it months earlier.

November   We sign a historic union agreement, ending arcane
2009   and absurd employee work rules and instituting a massive culture change.

March 2010   We complete the fiscal year with a fourth consecutive surplus, a sixth consecutive year of increased ridership, increased customer satisfaction, and improved productivity.

INDEX